MW00957090

ZURICH
TRAVEL GUIDE

Uncover the Allure and Heritage of Switzerland's Most Vibrant City

MILES LARKWOOD

All rights reserved. No part of this publication may be reproduced, distributed, or transmitted in any form or by any means, including photocopying, recording, or other electronic or mechanical methods, without the prior written permission of the publisher, except in the case of brief quotations embodied in critical reviews and certain other noncommercial uses permitted by copyright law.

Copyright © Miles Larkwood, 2024.

Table of Contents

PREFACE

Zurich isn't just a city; it's a journey through time, culture, and scenery that surprises at every turn. You may arrive expecting a financial hub or a place of pristine order, but what you'll discover is something far deeper and more alive. It's a city where centuries-old cobblestones meet the shimmer of modern skyscrapers, and where quiet lakeside strolls can transform into late-night adventures.

As you walk through the streets of Zurich, you'll find it hard to define. Is it the breathtaking sight of the Alps in the distance? The sound of church bells echoing in the Old Town? The hum of conversations in a cozy café as people linger over their espresso? Or is it the vibrancy of a summer festival or the stillness of a winter night by the lake?

There's something about Zurich that defies easy description—it's a place that feels both familiar and completely unexpected at the same time. My hope is that through this guide, you'll come to know this city not as a distant destination on a map, but as a place that invites you in, whether you're seeking history, art, adventure, or simply a moment of peace.

So come along, and let's explore the many sides of Zurich together. It's a city that will capture your heart, not because it demands your attention, but because it earns it in ways you won't see coming.

1

Overview Of The city

Zurich, Switzerland's largest city, is more than just a global financial hub—it's a blend of modern innovation, rich history, and natural beauty. Set against the backdrop of the snow-capped Alps, the city stretches along the northern shores of Lake Zurich, with the Limmat River cutting through its heart. Known for its high standard of living, efficient infrastructure, and cleanliness, Zurich consistently ranks as one of the best cities in the world to live in. For travelers, it's a destination that offers something for everyone, from history enthusiasts to art lovers, outdoor adventurers, and foodies alike.

Despite its reputation for being an economic powerhouse, Zurich exudes a laid-back charm that makes it equally appealing for leisure. The city's historical core, the Altstadt (Old Town), invites visitors to wander through medieval streets, past ancient churches, and into cozy cafes and boutiques. This is where Zurich's history comes alive, with buildings dating back to Roman times and landmarks like the Grossmünster and Fraumünster churches, whose towering spires dominate the skyline.

While Zurich embraces its past, it is also at the forefront of modernity. The city is home to the headquarters of numerous multinational corporations, including major banks and insurance companies, which contribute to its global financial influence. Yet, beyond this image of wealth and power lies a city that treasures its cultural heritage and constantly evolves to embrace the future. From cutting-edge architecture and sustainable urban planning to its thriving arts scene, Zurich is a city that refuses to be one-dimensional.

Geography and Natural Setting

One of the most striking aspects of Zurich is its natural surroundings. To the north, the city is framed by forested hills, while to the south, the clear blue waters of Lake Zurich stretch out, reflecting the distant peaks of the Alps. The nearby Uetliberg Mountain offers panoramic views of the city and its surroundings, and it's a favorite spot for both locals and tourists seeking a quiet escape into nature.

Lake Zurich is not just a beautiful sight, but also a hub for recreation. During the warmer months, the lake comes alive with swimmers, boaters, and sunbathers enjoying the clear water and public parks that line the shore. The city's residents are known for their active, outdoor lifestyles, and Zurich's numerous parks, including the expansive Zurichhorn and Belvoir Park, provide perfect green spaces to relax or engage in outdoor activities.

Historical and Cultural Significance

Zurich's roots trace back more than 2,000 years to Roman times, when it was known as Turicum, a customs post along the Limmat River. Over the centuries, it grew into a major center for trade, eventually becoming the prosperous city it is today. Throughout its long history, Zurich has managed to maintain a distinct identity, balancing its role as a global city with a strong sense of tradition.

In the medieval period, Zurich flourished under the rule of the Holy Roman Empire and later became part of the Swiss Confederation in the 14th century. The Protestant Reformation, led by Zurich's own Huldrych Zwingli in the 16th century, left a lasting impact on the city's religious and cultural landscape. Today, remnants of this rich history can be seen throughout the Old Town, from its churches to its well-preserved medieval buildings.

In addition to its historical significance, Zurich has long been a cultural hub. The city is home to some of Switzerland's most prestigious museums and galleries, including the Kunsthaus Zürich, which houses an impressive collection of Swiss and international art. Zurich has also played a key role in the development of modern art and literature. In the early 20th century, it was a center for the Dada movement, with famous artists and writers like Tristan Tzara and Hugo Ball gathering at the Cabaret Voltaire in Zurich to experiment with radical new forms of expression.

Today, Zurich continues to nurture creativity, with a vibrant arts and theater scene. The city hosts numerous cultural festivals, such as the Zurich Film Festival and Züri Fäscht, a large-scale celebration that brings together locals and tourists for parades, fireworks, and entertainment.

Modern Zurich

While Zurich's historical heart beats in the Old Town, the city's modern side is equally captivating. The Zurich-West district, once an industrial area, has transformed into a trendy neighborhood filled with hip restaurants, art galleries, and creative spaces. This area embodies Zurich's ability to reinvent itself while still preserving its core values. Visitors can explore modern architectural marvels like the Prime Tower, Switzerland's tallest building, or stroll through the converted warehouses now home to unique shops, art studios, and markets.

Zurich also embraces innovation in science and technology. The prestigious ETH Zurich (Swiss Federal Institute of Technology) is one of the world's leading universities in scientific research and innovation, having produced numerous Nobel laureates, including Albert Einstein. The university's presence helps maintain Zurich's status as a center for academic excellence and technological advancement.

Sustainability is another key element of modern Zurich. The city is a leader in eco-friendly living, with a strong focus on renewable energy, green public spaces, and efficient public transportation. Bicycles, trams, and electric buses are a common sight on Zurich's streets, and the city is committed to reducing its carbon footprint through various urban planning initiatives.

A City of Contrasts and Balance

What makes Zurich unique is its perfect balance of contrasts. It's a city where ancient history meets cutting-edge innovation, where tranquil natural beauty coexists with the buzz of urban life. Despite its small size compared to other global cities, Zurich offers a rich and diverse experience that caters to all kinds of travelers. Whether you're seeking the calm of nature, the excitement of the arts, or the pleasures of fine dining, Zurich promises to deliver in unexpected and delightful ways.

As the gateway to Switzerland, Zurich welcomes millions of visitors each year who come to experience its unique charm. Whether it's the awe-inspiring beauty of the surrounding mountains and lake, the deep-rooted sense of history, or the vibrant pulse of modern culture, Zurich captivates and inspires. In this guide, you'll discover the city's many faces and uncover the hidden gems that make Zurich an unforgettable destination.

History And Culture

Zurich's history stretches back over two millennia, and its cultural identity has been shaped by a series of pivotal moments. From its origins as a Roman customs station to its emergence as a significant political and economic center during the Middle Ages, Zurich has always held a key position in European history. However, it's the city's ability to adapt and innovate while preserving its heritage that has cemented its reputation as a cultural hub in Switzerland and beyond.

Roman Beginnings and Early Development

The history of Zurich begins with its foundation as Turicum, a small Roman settlement established around 15 B.C. Situated on the banks of the Limmat River, which connects Lake Zurich to the Rhine, Turicum served primarily as a tax collection point for goods transported along the river. The remnants of Roman structures, including a customs house, have been found in the area, offering a glimpse into Zurich's earliest days.

By the early medieval period, Zurich had grown into a fortified town under the Carolingian Empire, and its strategic location at the intersection of trade routes made it a flourishing center for commerce. By the 10th century, Zurich was an established royal town under Otto the Great, who played a crucial role in the city's growth.

Middle Ages: A City of Trade and Power

Zurich's importance increased in the Middle Ages when it became a free imperial city within the Holy Roman Empire. By the 14th century, it was a thriving commercial hub, bolstered by its textile industry, particularly the production of wool. Merchants from across Europe traded in Zurich, bringing wealth and influence to the city.

In 1351, Zurich joined the Swiss Confederation, becoming the fifth member of the alliance that would eventually lead to the formation of modern Switzerland. This period was marked by Zurich's rising political power in the region, and it became one of the most important cities in the Swiss Confederation. The city's strong walls, guilds, and mercantile spirit allowed it to play a significant role in Swiss politics and trade.

The Protestant Reformation: Zurich's Religious Revolution

One of the most defining periods in Zurich's history was the Protestant Reformation in the early 16th century, led by Huldrych Zwingli. Zwingli, a preacher at the Grossmünster church, is considered one of the leading figures of the Reformation alongside Martin Luther and John Calvin. His sermons in Zurich called for religious reforms, advocating for the removal of elaborate church decorations, the abolition of the Catholic Mass, and a return to the scriptures as the sole authority in Christian life.

Zwingli's influence quickly spread throughout Zurich and beyond, making the city one of the key centers of Protestantism in Europe. Under Zwingli's guidance, Zurich became a model for other Reformed cities, both religiously and politically. The Reformation's impact on Zurich was profound, affecting everything from the city's governance to its architecture, much of which reflected the new, stripped-back Protestant aesthetic.

Today, traces of the Reformation remain, especially in Zurich's churches. The Grossmünster, where Zwingli preached, stands as a symbol of this transformative era, while the Fraumünster, famous for its stained-glass windows by Marc Chagall, reflects the city's ongoing religious and artistic legacy.

19th and 20th Century Growth: Industrialization and Cultural Renaissance

The 19th century was a period of rapid growth and modernization for Zurich. The city embraced industrialization, which further boosted its economy. Textiles remained a major industry, but Zurich also became a center for machinery, engineering, and financial services, laying the groundwork for its eventual status as a global financial capital.

During this period, Zurich also became a hub for intellectuals, artists, and political thinkers. The founding of ETH Zurich (Swiss Federal Institute of Technology) in 1855 brought a flood of academic talent to the city, including Albert Einstein, who studied and later taught at the institution. The university continues to be one of the world's leading centers for science and technology.

The early 20th century saw Zurich take on a new role as a haven for artists and political exiles. During World War I, the city was neutral territory, and it attracted an influx of thinkers and writers from across Europe. Among these was the group of avant-garde artists who founded the Dada movement in 1916 at the Cabaret Voltaire. The Dadaists rejected traditional art forms and embraced absurdity and randomness as a response to the horrors of the war. Their influence would go on to shape modern art movements worldwide.

Modern Zurich: A Cultural Metropolis

Today, Zurich is known not only for its financial institutions but also for its rich cultural scene. The city is home to world-class museums, galleries, theaters, and concert halls that draw visitors from around the globe.

Kunsthaus Zürich, one of the most important art museums in Switzerland, houses an extensive collection of modern and contemporary works, including pieces by Swiss artists like Alberto Giacometti and Ferdinand Hodler, as well as international masters such as Picasso, Monet, and Chagall. Art lovers can also explore smaller galleries throughout the city, many of which are concentrated in Zurich-West, a once-industrial district that has transformed into a creative hub.

Music and theater also play a vital role in Zurich's cultural identity. The Tonhalle Zürich, one of Europe's leading concert halls, hosts world-renowned orchestras and soloists, while the Zurich Opera House stages performances of classical and modern operas. The city is also home to experimental theater, contemporary dance, and numerous film festivals, including the prestigious Zurich Film Festival, which attracts top talent from the international film industry.

Festivals and Traditions

Zurich celebrates its culture and traditions through a variety of festivals that showcase the city's heritage and creativity. One of the most popular is Zürifäscht, a massive public festival held every three years, which features fireworks, parades, concerts, and street performances. The event draws hundreds of thousands of visitors and is a true reflection of Zurich's festive spirit.

In winter, Zurich transforms into a magical wonderland with its Christmas markets, especially at Sechseläutenplatz and Bahnhofstrasse. These markets, filled with holiday lights, artisan stalls, and the smell of mulled wine, offer a glimpse into the Swiss holiday traditions that make this season so special.

Zurich also holds Sechseläuten, a traditional spring festival that symbolizes the end of winter. The festival culminates in the burning of a snowman effigy, known as the Böögg, which is said to predict how warm the summer will be based on how quickly it burns. It's a celebration that brings the entire city together and highlights Zurich's strong sense of community.

Cultural Diversity and Contemporary Life

Though Zurich has deep roots in Swiss tradition, it is also a cosmopolitan city with a diverse population. People from all over the world call Zurich home, contributing to its vibrant and multicultural atmosphere. This diversity is reflected in Zurich's food scene, where traditional Swiss dishes like fondue and raclette coexist with flavors from across the globe, including Italian, Turkish, Indian, and Japanese cuisine.

Zurich's neighborhoods each offer their own cultural vibe. From the chic, upscale shops and cafes of Seefeld to the trendy, alternative scene in Kreis 4, the city is a tapestry of different influences that blend together seamlessly. This combination of old and new, local and global, creates a cultural richness that makes Zurich one of Europe's most fascinating cities.

In conclusion, Zurich's history and culture are deeply intertwined, forming a city that honors its past while constantly looking to the future. Whether it's through its architecture, festivals, art, or culinary traditions, Zurich offers a cultural experience that is both profound and ever-evolving. As you explore its streets and landmarks, you'll find that Zurich is not just a place to visit—it's a place to experience.

2

Transportation Options: Flights, Trains, and Buses

Zurich, Switzerland's largest city, is one of Europe's major transportation hubs. It offers a variety of convenient and efficient transportation options for travelers arriving from all parts of the world. Whether you prefer to fly, take the train, or travel by bus, getting to Zurich is easy, comfortable, and well-connected. Here's an extensive overview of the transportation options available to reach Zurich.

Flights to Zurich

Zurich is home to Zurich Airport (Flughafen Zürich), the busiest international airport in Switzerland and one of the best airports in Europe in terms of efficiency, cleanliness, and passenger services. The airport is located just 13 kilometers (8 miles) north of Zurich's city center, making it incredibly convenient for travelers.

International Connectivity:

Zurich Airport is well-connected to major cities across Europe, North America, Asia, Africa, and the Middle East, making it one of the primary gateways to Switzerland. Major airlines, including Swiss International Air Lines (the national carrier), Lufthansa, British Airways, Air France, Emirates, Qatar Airways, and United Airlines, operate frequent flights to and from Zurich.

European travelers will find that Zurich is easily accessible through a variety of low-cost and legacy carriers, with direct flights from cities like London, Paris, Berlin, Amsterdam, and Rome. For intercontinental travelers, Zurich offers non-stop flights from cities such as New York, Los Angeles, Toronto, Dubai, and Singapore.

Airport Facilities and Transportation to the City:

Zurich Airport is renowned for its excellent facilities, including numerous shops, restaurants, duty-free stores, lounges, and passenger services. Upon landing, passengers have several efficient options for getting into Zurich's city center:

Train:
Zurich Airport is directly connected to the city's main train station (Zurich Hauptbahnhof, or Zurich HB) by a frequent and fast train service. Trains depart approximately every 10 minutes from the airport station, located beneath the terminal, and reach Zurich HB in just 10-15 minutes. This is by far the most popular and efficient way to get into the city from the airport.

Tram:
The Glattalbahn tram line 10 also provides a direct connection from the airport to Zurich's main train station. It's a slower option than the train, taking around 30-35 minutes, but it

offers a scenic route through suburban areas and is a comfortable option for those with large amounts of luggage.

Taxi:
Taxis are readily available outside the terminal and provide a more private but expensive option for getting into the city. A typical taxi ride from Zurich Airport to the city center takes about 20-30 minutes, depending on traffic, and costs around CHF 60-70.

Ride-Sharing:
Services like Uber are available at Zurich Airport and offer a more budget-friendly alternative to taxis.

Airlines and Destinations:

Zurich Airport serves as a hub for Swiss International Air Lines, which offers direct flights to over 80 destinations worldwide. Other major airlines that provide service to Zurich include:

Lufthansa:
Frequent flights from German cities like Frankfurt and Munich.

British Airways:
Daily flights from London and other UK cities.

Emirates:
Long-haul connections from Dubai.

Delta and United Airlines:
Direct flights from the U.S., including cities like New York, Atlanta, and Chicago.

Qatar Airways:
Direct flights from Doha, connecting to various Asian and Middle Eastern destinations.

Train Travel to Zurich

Traveling by train is one of the most scenic and comfortable ways to reach Zurich, especially if you're coming from other European cities. Switzerland's rail system is renowned for its punctuality, efficiency, and breathtaking routes through mountains, lakes, and valleys. Zurich is a key hub in the Swiss Federal Railways (SBB) network, and its Hauptbahnhof (Zurich HB) is the largest railway station in Switzerland.

From Switzerland and Neighboring Countries:

Switzerland's extensive and well-maintained rail network makes it easy to reach Zurich from almost any Swiss city or town. Whether you're traveling from Geneva, Basel, Lucerne, or Bern, you'll find frequent, fast trains to Zurich.

From Geneva:
Direct trains from Geneva Cornavin Station to Zurich HB take approximately 2 hours and 45 minutes, with several departures each hour.

From Lucerne:
Trains from Lucerne take about 45-50 minutes, making it an easy day trip or onward journey.

From Basel:
Direct trains from Basel SBB to Zurich HB take just over an hour.
International Trains:

Zurich is well-connected to neighboring countries through high-speed and intercity trains. EuroCity (EC), TGV Lyria, ICE (InterCity Express), and Railjet trains make international travel to Zurich both fast and comfortable.

From Germany:
Zurich has direct connections to major German cities such as Munich, Frankfurt, and Berlin via the ICE trains operated by Deutsche Bahn. Trains from Munich to Zurich, for example, take around 4 hours, while the journey from Frankfurt takes just 4 hours as well.

From France:
High-speed TGV Lyria trains connect Zurich with Paris in just over 4 hours. These trains are known for their comfort and speed, making Zurich an easy stop for travelers coming from France.

From Italy:
Zurich is easily accessible from northern Italy. Trenitalia and SBB operate direct trains from Milan to Zurich, with a journey time of just 3 hours and 30 minutes. The scenic route through the Alps via the Gotthard Base Tunnel offers breathtaking views, particularly during the winter months.

From Austria:
The Railjet trains operated by ÖBB connect Zurich with cities in Austria, such as Innsbruck and Vienna. The journey from Vienna to Zurich takes around 7 hours, making it a relaxing and scenic way to travel.

Train Facilities and Travel Experience:

Swiss trains are known for their punctuality and excellent service. They are equipped with comfortable seating, ample luggage space, free Wi-Fi on many routes, and food and drink services. Travelers in first class enjoy additional legroom, quiet coaches, and more personal space, making long-distance journeys particularly comfortable.

One of the biggest advantages of train travel in Switzerland is the scenery. Traveling by train offers stunning views of Switzerland's natural landscapes, from snow-capped mountains and rolling hills to pristine lakes and charming villages.

Bus Travel to Zurich

For budget-conscious travelers or those seeking an alternative to air or train travel, buses offer an affordable way to get to Zurich. Several international bus companies operate services to Zurich from various European cities.

Major Bus Operators:

FlixBus:
FlixBus is one of the largest and most popular long-distance bus operators in Europe, with numerous routes to Zurich from cities in Germany, France, Italy, Austria, and more. Buses are equipped with Wi-Fi, power outlets, and reclining seats, providing a comfortable journey at budget-friendly prices.

Eurolines:
Eurolines operates buses from cities like Paris, Brussels, and Amsterdam to Zurich. Their buses are similarly equipped with comfortable seating and basic amenities, making it a cost-effective option for travelers.

BlaBlaCar Bus:
Another low-cost bus operator, BlaBlaCar Bus (formerly known as Ouibus), connects Zurich with cities in France, Italy, and beyond.

Bus Terminals and Routes:

Buses arriving in Zurich typically stop at the Bus Terminal Zurich (Carparkplatz Sihlquai), located next to Zurich's main train station. This makes it easy for travelers to access public transport or continue their journey within Zurich.

Some popular routes include:

From Munich:
Buses from Munich to Zurich take around 4 to 5 hours, with several departures daily.

From Milan:
Buses from Milan to Zurich take about 4 to 5 hours, offering a budget-friendly alternative to train travel.

From Paris:
Buses from Paris to Zurich typically take 10 to 12 hours, depending on traffic and the number of stops along the way.

Travel Experience:

While bus travel may take longer than trains or flights, it offers flexibility and affordability. For travelers who don't mind longer journey times, buses are a great way to save money while still enjoying the comfort of modern transportation. Additionally, long-distance buses in Europe are often equipped with conveniences like air conditioning, free Wi-Fi, and USB charging ports, making the experience pleasant and convenient.

Whether you choose to fly, take the train, or travel by bus, Zurich is an easily accessible destination with a variety of transportation options to suit every traveler's needs. Its efficient airport, well-connected train network, and affordable bus services make it a convenient city to reach, no matter where you're coming from. Once you arrive, Zurich's excellent public transportation system ensures that you can explore the city with ease, making it an ideal starting point for your Swiss adventure.

Zurich's Efficient Public Transport System

Zurich's public transport system is renowned for its efficiency, punctuality, and extensive coverage. Managed by Zürcher Verkehrsverbund (ZVV), the network seamlessly integrates trams, trains, buses, boats, and even funiculars and cable cars. Whether you're navigating the city's bustling center or exploring its scenic outskirts, Zurich's public transport ensures that getting around is easy, fast, and reliable. Here's a detailed look at the components that make Zurich's public transport so effective and traveler-friendly.

Trams

Trams form the backbone of Zurich's public transportation system and are a familiar sight throughout the city. With over a dozen lines criss-crossing Zurich, the tram network offers extensive coverage, connecting passengers to nearly every corner of the city.

Key Features:

Frequent Service:
Trams run frequently, typically every 7-15 minutes during the day, with even more frequent service during peak hours.

Network Coverage:
The tram system covers popular districts like the Old Town (Altstadt), Zurich-West, and the University District, as well as key attractions like Lake Zurich and Bahnhofstrasse.

Accessibility:

Most trams are modern and accessible, with low-floor designs that accommodate passengers with strollers, luggage, or mobility challenges. Digital displays and announcements make it easy for visitors to navigate the system.

Tram service operates from early morning until midnight, with night services on weekends, ensuring transport is available at almost any hour.

Trains (S-Bahn)

The S-Bahn (suburban trains) is another essential part of Zurich's public transport network. While primarily used for regional travel, the S-Bahn also provides rapid connections within the city.

Key Features:

Main Station (Zurich HB):
All S-Bahn lines converge at Zurich Hauptbahnhof (Zurich HB), the city's central railway station and a major hub for domestic and international train services.

Quick City Access:
The S-Bahn is ideal for reaching destinations slightly outside the city center or exploring scenic areas around Zurich. For instance, S-Bahn trains can take you to popular spots like Uetliberg Mountain, which offers panoramic views of the city and surroundings.

Efficient Commuting:
S-Bahn trains run frequently, with services typically every 10-30 minutes, depending on the line and time of day.
Buses

Zurich's bus network complements the tram and S-Bahn systems, reaching areas that aren't directly accessible by other forms of public transport.

Key Features:

Extensive Coverage:
Buses connect neighborhoods beyond the reach of trams and trains, as well as key hubs like Zurich HB and Bellevue.

Integration with Other Transport:
Buses are fully integrated into the ZVV fare system, making it easy to switch between buses, trams, and trains on a single ticket.

Night Bus Services:
Zurich's night bus network operates on weekends, providing transportation between the city center and its outskirts late into the night.

Boats

Given Zurich's picturesque location on the shores of Lake Zurich, boat services offer both practicality and scenic enjoyment.

Key Features:

Lake Cruises and Ferries:
Regular ferry services operate between Zurich and nearby towns along Lake Zurich, such as Rapperswil and Thalwil. These ferries provide stunning views of the lake and surrounding mountains.

River Boats:
Smaller boats operate along the Limmat River, connecting the Swiss National Museum with Lake Zurich.

Boat services typically run from spring through autumn, making them a fantastic option during warmer months.

Funiculars and Cable Cars

Zurich's hilly terrain is part of its charm, and the city's funiculars and cable cars facilitate easy access to elevated viewpoints.

Key Features:

Polybahn:
This iconic funicular connects Central Square with the Swiss Federal Institute of Technology (ETH Zurich), offering great views along the way.

Rigiblick Funicular:
The Rigiblick connects the Zurich Zoo area to the Rigiblick neighborhood, providing stunning panoramas of Zurich and the surrounding countryside.

Dolderbahn:
This small rack railway connects the Römerhof district with the Dolder Grand hotel and nearby recreational areas.

Felsenegg Cable Car:
Departing from Adliswil, this cable car takes visitors to a ridge with breathtaking views and hiking trails.

Ticketing and Fares

Zurich's public transport system operates under the Zürcher Verkehrsverbund (ZVV), meaning the same ticket is valid for trams, buses, trains, and boats within the city's transportation zones. The fare system is based on zones, and prices vary depending on how many zones you travel through. Here's a breakdown of key ticketing options:

Single Tickets:
Valid for one journey within the designated zones.
Prices: Starting from approximately CHF 2.70 for 1 zone and CHF 4.40 for 2 zones, valid for 1 hour.

Day Passes:
Unlimited travel within Zurich for a full day.
Prices: Approximately CHF 8.80 for 1 zone and CHF 12.40 for 2 zones.

Zurich Card:
Unlimited travel on all public transport in Zurich and surrounding areas, as well as free or discounted admission to many museums and attractions.
Prices: Available for CHF 27 for 24 hours or CHF 53 for 72 hours.

Tickets can be purchased at ticket machines located at tram, bus, and train stations, or via the ZVV app. It's important to note that Zurich operates on an honor system; there are no ticket barriers, but random checks are frequent, and fines for traveling without a valid ticket can be substantial.

Punctuality and Reliability

Zurich's public transport is famous for its punctuality. Trains, trams, and buses typically adhere to their schedules, with digital displays at stations keeping passengers informed about arrival times. The ZVV app allows travelers to plan their journeys, check schedules, and buy tickets in real time.

Cycling and E-Scooters

While not part of the public transport network, Zurich is very bike-friendly, with numerous bike lanes throughout the city. Visitors can rent bikes or e-bikes through services like Züri rollt, a free bike rental service, or through private rental companies. Additionally, e-scooters are widely available for rent, providing a flexible and eco-friendly way to explore the city.

Zurich's public transport system is not only efficient but also a pleasure to use. With its seamless integration of trams, buses, trains, boats, and more, getting around the city and beyond is fast, comfortable, and scenic. Whether commuting between attractions in the heart of Zurich or venturing out into the surrounding countryside, the public transport system ensures that your travels are as smooth and enjoyable as possible.

Tips For Navigating The City

Navigating Zurich is relatively straightforward, thanks to its well-organized layout and efficient public transportation system. However, to make your visit even smoother, here are some practical tips that will help you get around the city like a local:

Understand the Zones and Tickets

Zurich's public transport system operates on a zone-based fare system. It's essential to know which zones you'll be traveling through, as ticket prices are based on the number of zones. Most tourist attractions are within Zone 110, which covers the central area of Zurich. However, if you're planning to visit places outside the city center, like the airport or Uetliberg Mountain, you'll need a ticket that covers additional zones.

Zurich HB (Main Station) is in Zone 110.
Zurich Airport is in Zone 121.

If you're planning a full day of sightseeing, a day pass or the Zurich Card might be more cost-effective. These passes allow unlimited travel within specified zones and often offer discounts at major attractions.

Buy Tickets Before Boarding

Public transport in Zurich operates on an honor system, meaning there are no barriers or gates to pass through when boarding trams, buses, or trains. However, you must buy your ticket before boarding, as ticket inspectors conduct random checks. You can purchase tickets from:

Ticket Machines:
Found at tram stops, bus stations, and train stations. They accept cash and credit cards.

ZVV App:
Download the ZVV app to buy tickets on your phone, plan routes, and check real-time schedules.

Failure to present a valid ticket during a check could result in a hefty fine (around CHF 100), so it's essential to always have a valid ticket.

Use the ZVV App for Real-Time Updates

Zurich's ZVV app is an indispensable tool for travelers. It provides real-time updates on tram, bus, and train schedules, maps of the public transport network, and even allows you to purchase tickets on the go. The app is available in multiple languages, including English, and is very user-friendly. You can also plan routes and check estimated travel times, making it easier to decide the quickest or most scenic route.

Avoid Rush Hour

Like most major cities, Zurich experiences rush hours during weekdays, particularly between 7:00 AM and 9:00 AM, and again from 4:30 PM to 6:30 PM. If you want to avoid packed trams and trains, try to schedule your travel outside of these peak times. Public transport is still punctual during rush hours, but the trams and buses may be crowded, especially on key routes.

Cycling Around Zurich

Zurich is a bike-friendly city, with dedicated bike lanes on many roads. If you enjoy cycling, consider renting a bike or e-bike. Services like Züri rollt provide free bike rentals at certain locations for short-term use, which is ideal for tourists. However, make sure to stay in the bike lanes and respect traffic signals, as Zurich's roads can be busy.

Tip:
Always lock your bike when not in use, as bike theft can be an issue in Zurich, just like in other major cities.

Walk When Possible

Zurich is a relatively compact city, especially in the downtown area, making it ideal for walking. Many of the city's most famous landmarks, like Bahnhofstrasse, Old Town (Altstadt), and Lake Zurich, are within walking distance of each other. Walking not only allows you to take in the city's beautiful architecture and scenic views, but it also helps you discover hidden gems like quaint cafés, boutiques, and charming alleyways.

Tip:
Wear comfortable shoes, as some areas of Zurich, particularly in the Old Town, have cobblestone streets.

Navigating Zurich HB (Main Station)

Zurich HB, the city's central railway station, can feel overwhelming due to its size and constant activity. The station serves as a hub for trains, trams, and buses, with numerous shops, restaurants, and service points.

Tip:
If you're transferring between transport modes at Zurich HB, give yourself plenty of time, as it can take a few minutes to navigate between platforms, tram stops, or bus terminals.

Look for Signage:
Zurich HB is well signposted, with clear directions in both German and English. Look for the large digital screens that display the schedules for trains, trams, and buses.

Use Google Maps for Walking and Public Transport

While the ZVV app is excellent for public transport, Google Maps is also a great tool for navigating Zurich, especially if you're walking. The app provides accurate directions and travel times for both public transport and walking routes. You can also use it to search for nearby attractions, restaurants, and shops.

Learn Some Basic German Phrases

Although Zurich is a global city where many people speak English, learning a few basic German phrases can make navigating the city easier and more enjoyable. Simple greetings like "Guten Morgen" (Good morning) or "Danke" (Thank you) are always appreciated, especially when interacting with locals.

Here are a few useful phrases:
- Fahrkarte, bitte: A ticket, please.
- Wie viel kostet das?: How much does it cost?

- Entschuldigung, wo ist der Bahnhof?: Excuse me, where is the train station?

Stay Aware of Quiet Zones

Some trams and trains in Zurich have designated quiet zones, where passengers are expected to keep noise to a minimum. If you enter one of these zones, marked by a "quiet zone" symbol, remember to keep conversations to a low volume and avoid making phone calls. These areas are perfect for resting after a day of exploring the city or for reading a book during a peaceful ride.

Watch Out for Cyclists

While Zurich is highly walkable, it's essential to be mindful of cyclists. Bike lanes are common, particularly along the lake and major streets, and cyclists have the right of way. Always look both ways before crossing a bike lane, and stick to pedestrian areas when walking.

Zurich is one of the most traveler-friendly cities in the world, and with a bit of preparation, getting around is a breeze. Whether you're using public transport, walking, or cycling, you'll find Zurich easy to navigate. Keep these tips in mind to ensure that your time in the city is as enjoyable and stress-free as possible.

3

Historic Landmarks And Architecture

Zurich's Old Town, or Altstadt, is the heart of the city, both geographically and historically. Walking through its narrow, cobblestone streets feels like stepping back in time, with every corner revealing centuries-old buildings, medieval towers, and charming squares. This district is where Zurich's roots as a Roman settlement and medieval trading post come to life, and it's here that you'll encounter many of the city's most iconic historic landmarks and architectural gems.

Grossmünster (Great Minster)

One of Zurich's most famous landmarks, the Grossmünster is a Romanesque-style Protestant church that dates back to the 12th century. According to legend, the church was founded by Charlemagne, who supposedly discovered the graves of Zurich's patron saints, Felix and Regula, on the site.

Key Features:

Twin Towers:
The Grossmünster's twin towers are a defining feature of Zurich's skyline. Climbing the towers offers a rewarding panoramic view of the city, Lake Zurich, and the distant Alps.

Romanesque Architecture:
The church's Romanesque architecture, with its heavy stone walls, semi-circular arches, and simple yet imposing design, reflects the religious and cultural climate of the time.

Reformation History:
The Grossmünster played a key role in the Swiss Reformation, led by Huldrych Zwingli in the early 16th century. Today, it remains a symbol of Zurich's Protestant heritage.

Inside, the church features stunning stained-glass windows designed by the renowned Swiss artist Augusto Giacometti, as well as a crypt that holds the remains of Felix and Regula.

Fraumünster Church

Just across the river from Grossmünster lies the Fraumünster Church, another historic site with deep roots in Zurich's past. Founded in 853 by Emperor Louis the German for his daughter Hildegard, Fraumünster was originally a convent for aristocratic women. Over the centuries, it evolved into one of Zurich's most important churches.

Key Features:

Chagall Windows:
The highlight of the Fraumünster Church is its five large stained-glass windows, created by the famed Russian-French artist Marc Chagall in 1970. Each window tells a different biblical story in vibrant, dreamlike colors, making the church an artistic pilgrimage for visitors.

Gothic and Romanesque Architecture:

While the original structure dates back to the 9th century, much of what you see today was built in the 13th and 15th centuries. The church features a mix of Romanesque and Gothic styles, with pointed arches, ribbed vaults, and a stunningly simple yet elegant interior.

Munsterhof Square:
The church is situated near Münsterhof, a picturesque square that was once the convent's courtyard. Today, it's a tranquil spot in the Old Town, perfect for taking in the beauty of the surrounding historic architecture.

St. Peter's Church

St. Peter's Church is another iconic Zurich landmark, known for having the largest church clock face in Europe, with a diameter of over 8.5 meters (28 feet). The church stands on a site that has been a place of worship since Roman times, though the current structure dates back to the early 13th century.

Key Features:

Clock Tower:
The giant clock face is the standout feature of St. Peter's Church, and its hourly chimes are a familiar sound in Zurich's Old Town. The clock has been keeping time for Zurich's residents for over 500 years.

Romanesque Architecture:
While the church was extensively remodeled during the Baroque period, parts of the original Romanesque structure remain, especially in the choir and crypt areas.

Burials of Prominent Figures:
Several prominent Zurich figures, including Johann Caspar Lavater, the famed philosopher and theologian, are buried here. Inside, visitors can also find a series of fascinating medieval frescoes and carvings.

Lindenhof Hill

Lindenhof Hill is one of Zurich's most historically significant locations. It was here that the Romans established a customs post in the 1st century BC, and later, it became the site of a Carolingian royal residence. Today, Lindenhof offers more than just history—it provides stunning views of Zurich's cityscape, the Limmat River, and the Alps.

Key Features:

Historic Site:
In the 9th century, Zurich's first fortified castle was built on Lindenhof, and the area later became a gathering place for important civic events, including the swearing of Zurich's constitution in 1798.

Scenic Viewpoint:
Lindenhof's location atop a hill makes it one of the best spots in the city to enjoy panoramic views. From here, you can see Zurich's Old Town, the spires of the Grossmünster, and the Limmat River meandering through the city.

Quiet Oasis:
Despite its historical significance, Lindenhof remains a peaceful and relatively quiet spot. Locals often come here to relax, play chess, or enjoy a break from the hustle and bustle of the city.

Niederdorf (Old Town District)

The Niederdorf is one of the liveliest and most atmospheric parts of Zurich's Old Town. This pedestrianized area is filled with narrow streets, hidden squares, and medieval buildings. It's a place where history meets modern life, as the old-world charm is balanced by a variety of trendy cafés, restaurants, and boutiques.

Key Features:

Medieval Streets:
Niederdorf's winding streets are a joy to explore, offering a mix of medieval architecture and charming facades. Keep an eye out for Rennweg and Augustinergasse, two of the most picturesque streets in the district.

Boutiques and Cafés:
While exploring, you'll find plenty of small shops and cafés tucked into the medieval buildings, making it a great place for shopping or a leisurely coffee break.

Nightlife:
At night, the Niederdorf area comes alive with vibrant bars and music venues. While it retains its historic charm, this part of the Old Town is also one of Zurich's best nightlife spots.

The Town Hall (Rathaus)

Zurich's Rathaus (Town Hall) is a magnificent Baroque structure that has served as the seat of the city's government since the late 17th century. Located along the Limmat River, the Rathaus is an important political and historical building, as it hosted many key meetings during the Reformation and beyond.

Key Features:

Baroque Architecture:
Built between 1694 and 1698, Zurich's Town Hall is one of the city's finest examples of Baroque architecture. The stone façade is grand yet elegant, with decorative cornices and arched windows adding to its stately appearance.

Interior:
While the building is still used for governmental functions, visitors can often enter the Rathaus to admire its historic interior. Inside, you'll find richly decorated rooms with wood-paneled walls and large murals that tell Zurich's political and religious history.

Guild Houses (Zunfthäuser)

In Zurich, the influence of the guilds (Zünfte) can still be felt today. During the Middle Ages, these powerful merchant and artisan guilds controlled much of the city's political and economic life. Many of the historic guild houses still stand in the Old Town, each one representing a different craft or trade.

Key Features:

Rennweg and Limmatquai:
Two of the main streets in the Old Town where you can spot the grand guild houses. The Haus zum Rüden, for example, represents the guild of noblemen, while the Haus zur Meisen is an impressive Baroque building now housing the Swiss Porcelain Museum.

Sechseläutenplatz:
This square near the Old Town is the site of the Sechseläuten festival, where Zurich's guilds parade in traditional dress before burning the Böögg, a snowman effigy symbolizing winter.

Zurich's Old Town is an architectural and historical treasure trove, where centuries of history unfold as you explore its winding streets and towering landmarks. Whether you're admiring the grandeur of the Grossmünster, relaxing on Lindenhof Hill, or delving into the rich history of the city's guilds, Altstadt offers a journey through Zurich's past that is both captivating and enriching.

Key Attractions: Grossmünster, Fraumünster, And Lindenhof

Grossmünster

The Grossmünster is an imposing and majestic structure with its twin towers rising above Zurich's skyline. Known as the birthplace of the Swiss Reformation, this Protestant church is steeped in historical and religious significance. Founded in the 12th century, it's tied to the legendary discovery of the graves of Zurich's patron saints, Felix and Regula, by Charlemagne himself.

The Grossmünster is not only an emblem of Zurich's spiritual life but also a remarkable architectural marvel. Its Romanesque design, characterized by solid stone walls and rounded arches, reflects the austerity of the era in which it was built. The church's exterior is relatively simple, but its twin towers are a defining feature of Zurich's cityscape. Visitors are encouraged to climb the Karlsturm (south tower), where they are rewarded with breathtaking views over Zurich, the Limmat River, and the distant snow-capped Alps.

Inside the Grossmünster, you'll find stunning stained-glass windows by Augusto Giacometti, whose modern designs provide a vivid contrast to the church's ancient stone walls. His windows infuse the church with light and color, creating an uplifting atmosphere within the otherwise austere setting. The crypt below holds historical significance, believed to be the burial place of Saints Felix and Regula.

In addition to its architectural and artistic highlights, the Grossmünster has played a crucial role in Zurich's religious history. Huldrych Zwingli, the leader of the Swiss Reformation, preached here in the early 16th century, ushering in a wave of Protestant reform that transformed not just Zurich but the wider Swiss Confederation. The Grossmünster remains a powerful symbol of the city's Protestant heritage and stands as a testament to Zurich's role in shaping the religious landscape of Europe.

Fraumünster

While the Grossmünster represents Zurich's Protestant history, the Fraumünster Church is equally important for its artistic legacy and its role in Zurich's early religious life. Originally founded as a convent for aristocratic women in 853 by Emperor Louis the German, the Fraumünster became a center of power and influence throughout the Middle Ages. The abbess of the convent wielded considerable authority, both religious and political, making the Fraumünster one of the most important institutions in Zurich's history.

Architecturally, the Fraumünster is a mix of Romanesque and Gothic styles, with tall, pointed arches and a vaulted ceiling that give the church a sense of grandeur. However, the true highlight of the Fraumünster is its stained-glass windows, particularly those created by the renowned artist Marc Chagall in 1970. These five large windows depict biblical scenes in vibrant blues, greens, and reds, with Chagall's characteristic dreamlike style. The central window, known as the Christ Window, portrays Christ surrounded by the prophets, while other windows depict events such as Jacob's Dream and Moses Receiving the Ten Commandments.

In addition to the Chagall windows, the Fraumünster also features a stunning choir window designed by Augusto Giacometti, which complements Chagall's work. These artistic masterpieces make the Fraumünster not just a place of worship but also a destination for art lovers. Visitors can sit in the peaceful, light-filled nave and contemplate the stories and emotions depicted in the stained glass, which adds an element of beauty and reflection to any visit.

The Münsterhof Square in front of the Fraumünster, once the courtyard of the convent, is another highlight of the area. This picturesque square, surrounded by medieval buildings, offers a quiet place to sit and admire the historic surroundings.

Lindenhof

Lindenhof is a serene and historically significant park that offers one of the most spectacular viewpoints in Zurich. Situated on a hill in the heart of the Old Town, Lindenhof has been a gathering place for centuries. Its history dates back to Roman times, when it was the site of a Roman customs post and fort. Later, it became the location of a Carolingian royal residence, and it remained an important civic space throughout Zurich's history.

Though today it is a peaceful park, Lindenhof's past is marked by key historical events. In 1798, it was here that the citizens of Zurich swore an oath to the Helvetic Republic, a pivotal moment in Swiss history. The hill also offers a reminder of Zurich's medieval past, with remnants of ancient walls and other archaeological finds.

For visitors, Lindenhof's primary draw is its panoramic views of the city. From the top of the hill, you can see across the

Limmat River, taking in the red-tiled rooftops of Zurich's Old Town, the spires of the Grossmünster and Fraumünster, and the lush greenery that surrounds the city. On a clear day, the distant Alps provide a stunning backdrop to the urban landscape.

In addition to its historical significance, Lindenhof is a popular spot for both locals and tourists seeking a tranquil escape from the busy streets below. Locals often come to play chess on the outdoor boards, relax under the shade of the trees, or simply enjoy the view. It's also a favorite spot for photographers, who flock to the hill to capture the beauty of Zurich from above.

Lindenhof is free to visit, and it's an ideal place to pause, take in the surroundings, and reflect on the centuries of history that have unfolded on this very hill.

The Grossmünster, Fraumünster, and Lindenhof are three of the most important landmarks in Zurich, each offering a unique window into the city's past. The Grossmünster represents Zurich's religious and political transformation during the Reformation, while the Fraumünster is a testament to the city's artistic heritage, thanks to its stunning stained-glass windows. Meanwhile, Lindenhof provides a peaceful space to reflect on Zurich's ancient history while enjoying breathtaking views of the city. Together, these attractions form the cultural and historical backbone of Zurich's Old Town, making them essential stops for any visitor looking to truly understand and appreciate the city.

Best Cafés, Shops, And Hidden Gems in Altstadt

Zurich's Old Town, known as Altstadt, is a charming maze of narrow cobblestone streets, historic landmarks, and delightful spots to relax and explore. Here are some top recommendations:

Café Bar ODEON:
A historic café that has been a gathering place for artists and intellectuals since the early 20th century. Enjoy classic Swiss pastries and coffee in an elegant setting.

Babu's Bakery & Coffeehouse:
Renowned for its freshly baked goods and cozy atmosphere, Babu's offers a perfect spot to unwind with a cup of coffee and a slice of homemade cake.

Confiserie Sprüngli:
A paradise for chocolate lovers, this iconic shop offers a wide array of Swiss chocolates and confections, making it an ideal place to find sweet souvenirs.

Boutique Roma:
A family-run boutique offering a curated selection of Swiss-made clothing and accessories, blending traditional craftsmanship with modern fashion.

Lindenhof:
A peaceful hilltop park providing panoramic views of the city. It's a favorite among locals and visitors alike for picnics and relaxation.

Moulagenmuseum:

For those interested in medical history, this museum showcases a unique collection of wax models depicting various diseases and injuries, offering a glimpse into the past.

These establishments and spots encapsulate the essence of Zurich's Old Town, offering a blend of history, culture, and local flavor.

4

Kunsthaus Zürich And Modern Art Galleries

Zurich is a vibrant cultural hub, renowned for its rich art scene that spans centuries. From classical masterpieces to contemporary installations, the city offers an array of artistic experiences, with the Kunsthaus Zürich at its center. Zurich's galleries and museums attract art lovers from around the world, offering an in-depth look at both traditional and modern art movements. In this section, we will explore the Kunsthaus Zürich and other significant modern art galleries, showcasing Zurich's diverse and dynamic artistic landscape.

Kunsthaus Zürich: The Heart of Zurich's Art Scene

The Kunsthaus Zürich is the most prominent art museum in the city and one of the leading art institutions in Switzerland. Founded in 1910, it houses an extensive collection of works from the Middle Ages to contemporary art, making it a must-visit for anyone interested in exploring Zurich's artistic heritage.

Permanent Collection:
The Kunsthaus is renowned for its vast and varied permanent collection. Some of the key highlights include:

Old Masters:
The museum's collection begins with European art from the Middle Ages and Renaissance periods. Among the notable works are paintings by Rembrandt, Rubens, and Titian, showcasing the skills and techniques of the masters who shaped European art history.

Swiss Art:
One of the most important aspects of the Kunsthaus's collection is its focus on Swiss artists. The museum features a large selection of works by Alberto Giacometti, whose distinctive sculptures and paintings made him one of the most influential figures in 20th-century art. The Kunsthaus Zürich holds the largest collection of his works in the world, including his iconic elongated bronze sculptures and expressive portraits. Additionally, the museum showcases works by other Swiss artists, such as Félix Vallotton, Johann Heinrich Füssli, and Arnold Böcklin, whose mythological and symbolic works remain widely admired.

Impressionism and Post-Impressionism:
Visitors to the Kunsthaus Zürich can also enjoy an impressive selection of paintings from the Impressionist and Post-Impressionist periods. Noteworthy artists such as Claude Monet, Edgar Degas, Pierre-Auguste Renoir, and Vincent van Gogh are represented, with works that highlight the evolution of modern painting from the late 19th century.

Modernism:
The Kunsthaus is home to several pivotal works from early 20th-century movements, including Cubism, Surrealism, and Expressionism. Visitors can see pieces by Pablo Picasso, Georges Braque, Marc Chagall, and Joan Miró, who were key figures in redefining the boundaries of visual art.

Contemporary Art:
The museum also has a strong focus on contemporary art, with a significant collection of works by modern artists such as Gerhard Richter, Andy Warhol, Francis Bacon, and David Hockney. These pieces demonstrate the diversity and experimentation that characterize modern and postmodern art.

Special Exhibitions:
In addition to its permanent collection, the Kunsthaus Zürich regularly hosts temporary exhibitions that explore a wide range of themes and artistic movements. These exhibitions often feature works on loan from international museums and

private collections, offering visitors a chance to see rare and important pieces. The exhibitions range from retrospectives of individual artists to thematic shows that highlight specific periods or styles.

New Extension:
In 2021, the Kunsthaus Zürich underwent a major expansion, making it Switzerland's largest art museum. The new building, designed by renowned architect David Chipperfield, nearly doubled the museum's exhibition space and enhanced the museum's ability to host large-scale international exhibitions. The expansion also includes a new café, bookstore, and educational spaces, making it a more comprehensive cultural destination.

Zurich's Modern Art Galleries

While the Kunsthaus Zürich is the city's largest and most prominent museum, Zurich is also home to a vibrant contemporary art scene, with numerous galleries showcasing cutting-edge works by both Swiss and international artists.
Galerie Eva Presenhuber:

Galerie Eva Presenhuber is one of Zurich's leading contemporary art galleries, representing a roster of influential international artists. Located in the Löwenbräu district, which is a hub for contemporary art in Zurich, the gallery regularly hosts exhibitions featuring works by artists such as Ugo Rondinone, Tobias Pils, and Doug Aitken.

The gallery focuses on showcasing artists who work in a variety of media, from painting and sculpture to video and installation art. Galerie Eva Presenhuber has earned a reputation for presenting bold and innovative exhibitions, making it a must-visit for contemporary art enthusiasts.

Hauser & Wirth:

Hauser & Wirth, an internationally acclaimed gallery with locations in major cities around the world, has a strong presence in Zurich. Founded in 1992 by Iwan Wirth and Ursula Hauser, the gallery is known for its commitment to contemporary art and its representation of some of the most important living artists. The Zurich location regularly features exhibitions by artists such as Louise Bourgeois, Martin Creed, Annie Leibovitz, and Paul McCarthy.

Hauser & Wirth's exhibitions often explore challenging and thought-provoking themes, making it a key destination for visitors who want to engage with contemporary art that pushes boundaries.

LUMA Westbau:

Located within the Löwenbräu Art Complex, LUMA Westbau is an exhibition space dedicated to contemporary art and culture. Part of the larger LUMA Foundation, which supports artistic projects worldwide, LUMA Westbau features innovative exhibitions that blend art with social and environmental issues.

The gallery focuses on interdisciplinary projects, often involving collaborations between artists, scientists, and cultural thinkers. Its exhibitions explore topics such as sustainability, digital culture, and the relationship between art and technology, making it a space for cutting-edge, forward-thinking art.

Karma International:

Karma International is a Zurich-based gallery that has built a reputation for supporting emerging and mid-career artists. The gallery is known for its focus on experimental and conceptual art, with exhibitions that often challenge traditional notions of art-making.

The artists represented by Karma International work in a variety of media, including painting, sculpture, photography, and performance. The gallery regularly participates in international art fairs, helping to bring Zurich's contemporary art scene to a global audience.

Migros Museum of Contemporary Art:

Another essential stop for contemporary art lovers is the Migros Museum of Contemporary Art, also located in the Löwenbräu Art Complex. Established in 1996, the museum is part of the Migros Culture Percentage, a philanthropic initiative by the Swiss supermarket chain to promote the arts.

The Migros Museum is known for its innovative exhibitions, which often explore the intersections of art, society, and politics. Its collection includes works by contemporary artists such as John Baldessari, Mona Hatoum, and Pipilotti Rist, many of whom are known for their socially engaged and politically charged works.

The museum also hosts temporary exhibitions that focus on current trends in contemporary art, often featuring younger or lesser-known artists who are pushing the boundaries of their respective media.

Zurich's art scene is both deeply rooted in tradition and forward-looking, with the Kunsthaus Zürich serving as the city's artistic epicenter. The museum's extensive collection, ranging from medieval to contemporary works, offers a comprehensive look at the development of European and Swiss art. Meanwhile, Zurich's many modern art galleries, such as Galerie Eva Presenhuber, Hauser & Wirth, and the Migros Museum of Contemporary Art, ensure that the city remains at the cutting edge of the global art world. Whether you're a fan of classical masterpieces or bold contemporary installations, Zurich's art institutions provide a rich and diverse experience for all art lovers.

The Swiss National Museum

The Swiss National Museum (Landesmuseum Zürich) is one of Switzerland's most important cultural institutions and a must-visit destination for those interested in Swiss history, culture, and heritage. Located near Zurich's main train station (Hauptbahnhof), the museum offers a fascinating journey through the country's past, from prehistoric times to the present day. Housed in a striking neo-Gothic building, the museum blends history with modern design, providing an immersive experience for visitors of all ages.

History of the Swiss National Museum

The Swiss National Museum was established in 1898 and has since become one of the premier institutions for Swiss history and cultural studies. Its impressive building, designed by Gustav Gull, is reminiscent of a medieval castle, complete with turrets, towers, and a picturesque courtyard. The architecture itself is a blend of historical and romantic styles, reflecting Switzerland's rich past.

The museum is part of the Swiss National Museum group, which also includes the Château de Prangins and the Forum of Swiss History in Schwyz. Together, these institutions preserve and display Switzerland's cultural and historical heritage.

Permanent Exhibitions

The Swiss National Museum's permanent exhibitions cover a wide range of topics, offering insight into Switzerland's unique history, diverse cultures, and national identity.

Prehistoric and Early History:
The museum's collection starts with exhibits from Switzerland's prehistoric period, including Stone Age tools, Bronze Age artifacts, and items from Celtic and Roman times. Visitors can see ancient weapons, pottery, and jewelry that provide insight into the daily life of Switzerland's earliest inhabitants. There are also exhibits on the Roman Empire's influence in Switzerland, particularly focusing on the Roman settlements in Augusta Raurica and Vindonissa.

Middle Ages:
The Middle Ages played a crucial role in shaping Switzerland's identity, and this period is extensively covered in the museum. Highlights include displays on medieval Swiss knights, religious artifacts, and stunning examples of Gothic art and sculpture. The museum also showcases weapons and armor used during the era, providing insight into the conflicts and alliances that shaped medieval Switzerland.

Swiss Confederation:
One of the museum's most significant exhibits focuses on the formation and development of the Swiss Confederation, a crucial chapter in Swiss history. This section includes documents from the early Federal Charters, medieval battle standards, and relics from pivotal events such as the Battle of Morgarten (1315) and the Old Swiss Confederacy's independence. The exhibit traces the evolution of Switzerland's political system from a loose confederation of states to the modern federal republic that exists today.

Religious Reformation:
The Swiss National Museum also explores the impact of the Reformation on Switzerland, particularly the work of

Huldrych Zwingli, who led the Protestant Reformation in Zurich. The religious and social upheaval of the time is portrayed through historical documents, religious manuscripts, and artifacts from the 16th century. Visitors can learn how the Reformation shaped Switzerland's political landscape and contributed to its reputation for religious tolerance.

Swiss Cultural Traditions:
Another highlight of the museum is its focus on Swiss cultural traditions and customs. Exhibits on folk art, regional costumes, and traditional crafts like wood carving, weaving, and clockmaking provide insight into the everyday lives of Swiss people over the centuries. The museum's extensive collection of Swiss furniture and household items illustrates the evolution of Swiss domestic life.

Switzerland and the World:
This section delves into Switzerland's relationships with its European neighbors and the broader world. The exhibit explores Switzerland's role in international diplomacy, its tradition of neutrality, and its humanitarian contributions through organizations such as the Red Cross, which was founded in Geneva. Visitors can also learn about Switzerland's global economic influence and its status as a center for banking and commerce.

Special Exhibitions

The Swiss National Museum regularly hosts special exhibitions that focus on various aspects of Swiss history and culture, as well as broader international themes. These temporary exhibits often include rare artifacts, multimedia presentations, and interactive displays that engage visitors in new ways. Recent exhibitions have covered topics such as Swiss fashion, design, and innovations in science and technology.

Modern Museum Features

In addition to its historical exhibits, the Swiss National Museum has embraced modern technology to enhance the visitor experience. The museum's interactive displays, audio guides, and multimedia presentations make it easier for visitors to explore complex topics, from Swiss art history to political developments. The museum also features virtual reality experiences, allowing visitors to immerse themselves in historical events or explore ancient Swiss cities as they once were.

The museum's renovation and expansion in 2016 added a sleek modern wing, designed by the architects Christ & Gantenbein. This new space blends seamlessly with the original building and provides additional exhibition rooms, a café, and a gift shop. The modern wing also houses temporary exhibitions and events, creating a dynamic cultural hub in the heart of Zurich.

Visitor Information and Tips

Location:
The Swiss National Museum is located at Museumstrasse 2, just a short walk from Zurich's main train station (Zurich Hauptbahnhof). Its central location makes it easily accessible for visitors arriving by train, tram, or bus.
Opening Hours:

The museum is generally open from 10:00 AM to 5:00 PM, with extended hours on Thursdays until 7:00 PM. It is closed on Mondays, so plan accordingly.

Admission:
Adults: CHF 10-15 (depending on exhibitions)
Students and Seniors: Reduced rates
Children under 16: Free admission
Entry to special exhibitions may carry additional fees, and there are discounts for group visits.

Museum Tours:
The Swiss National Museum offers guided tours for visitors who want a deeper understanding of Swiss history and the exhibits on display. There are also self-guided audio tours available in multiple languages, including English, German, and French.

Museum Café and Shop:
After exploring the museum, visitors can relax at the on-site Café Spitz, which offers a variety of Swiss and international dishes in a stylish setting. The museum shop is also worth a visit, offering books, souvenirs, and unique Swiss-made products.

The Swiss National Museum is a treasure trove of Swiss history and culture, offering visitors a comprehensive look at the country's past, present, and future. Its diverse exhibitions cover everything from ancient history and medieval warfare to contemporary design and Swiss traditions. Whether you're interested in art, politics, or Swiss daily life, the museum provides an engaging and educational experience for all ages. The blend of traditional exhibits with modern, interactive elements ensures that every visitor can find something of interest, making the Swiss National Museum an essential stop on any visit to Zurich.

Zurich's theaters and Music Scene

Zurich is not only known for its picturesque landscapes and rich history, but it also boasts a vibrant theater and music scene that attracts both locals and visitors alike. From world-class opera and classical concerts to contemporary theater and experimental performances, Zurich offers a diverse range of cultural experiences. This section explores the city's major theaters, concert halls, and music venues, highlighting the dynamic artistic community that thrives here.

Zurich Opera House (Zürcher Oper)

The Zurich Opera House is one of the premier opera houses in Europe and a cornerstone of the city's cultural life. Opened in 1891, the stunning building, designed by architects Karl Moser and Robert G. Bär, features a magnificent neoclassical façade and an opulent interior, making it a true architectural gem.

Performances:
The opera house hosts a variety of performances throughout the year, including opera, ballet, and orchestral concerts. The Zurich Opera is known for its high-quality productions, featuring both classic works by composers such as Mozart, Verdi, and Wagner, as well as contemporary operas. The ballet company, which is one of the leading ballet troupes in the world, performs a diverse repertoire ranging from classical ballets to modern choreography.

Special Events:
In addition to regular performances, the Zurich Opera House often hosts special events, including galas and guest

1895, features stunning acoustics and elegant architecture. The Tonhalle hosts a diverse range of performances, including classical concerts, contemporary music, and special events. Regularly featuring both Swiss and international guest artists, the venue is a key player in the European classical music scene.

Moods:
Located in the trendy Zürich-West district, Moods is one of the best venues for jazz and world music in Zurich. The intimate club atmosphere attracts both local and international musicians, making it a hotspot for live performances. Moods also hosts jam sessions and workshops, fostering a sense of community among musicians and music lovers alike.

Helsinki Klub:
This cozy venue is known for showcasing indie and alternative music. With its laid-back atmosphere and eclectic lineup, Helsinki Klub provides a platform for both local and international bands to perform. The venue often features a mix of genres, from rock and pop to electronic music, ensuring that there's always something new and exciting to discover.

Zurich Openair Festival:
One of the most significant music festivals in Switzerland, the Zurich Openair Festival takes place every August and features a lineup of top international and local acts across various genres. Held in the expansive Zurich Altstetten area, the festival attracts thousands of music lovers for four days of live performances, food, and cultural activities. With stages set against a backdrop of the city skyline, it's a must-visit event for anyone wanting to experience Zurich's vibrant music scene.

Street Music:
In addition to formal venues, Zurich's streets and public squares come alive with street performances and busking. Local musicians, from classical violinists to indie rock bands, can often be found performing in popular areas like Bahnhofstrasse and Lindenhof, adding to the city's lively atmosphere.

Cultural Festivals and Events

Zurich's cultural calendar is packed with festivals that celebrate theater, music, and the arts. Some notable events include:

Zurich Film Festival:
Held annually in September, this festival showcases international films, documentaries, and short films, attracting filmmakers and cinema enthusiasts from around the globe. The festival often includes premieres, panels, and workshops, making it a key event in Zurich's cultural calendar.

Zürich Festival:
This city-wide festival occurs every summer and celebrates the performing arts, with theater, dance, music, and multimedia performances taking place in various venues throughout the city. It showcases both local talent and international artists, creating a lively atmosphere filled with creativity and innovation.

JazzNoJazz Festival:
A highlight for jazz enthusiasts, this festival takes place in November and features performances by renowned jazz musicians and bands from around the world. The festival

spans multiple venues in Zurich and celebrates the diversity of jazz music through concerts, workshops, and jam sessions.

Zurich's theaters and music scene reflect the city's rich cultural heritage and commitment to artistic innovation. With renowned venues like the Zurich Opera House and the Tonhalle, as well as a diverse range of theaters and music clubs, visitors can immerse themselves in a wide array of performances and concerts. Whether you are a fan of opera, contemporary theater, or live music, Zurich offers something for everyone, making it a vibrant hub for the arts that continues to inspire and entertain.

5

Bahnhofstrasse Luxury Brands And Boutiques

Bahnhofstrasse is not just a street; it's a symbol of Zurich's status as a global financial center and a mecca for luxury shopping. Stretching approximately 1.4 kilometers from Zurich Hauptbahnhof (main train station) to Lake Zurich, Bahnhofstrasse is lined with some of the world's most prestigious brands, exclusive boutiques, and elegant cafés. It is consistently ranked among the most expensive shopping streets globally, making it a must-visit destination for both shoppers and those interested in experiencing Zurich's high-end lifestyle.

A Stroll Down Bahnhofstrasse

Walking along Bahnhofstrasse is an experience in itself. The wide boulevard is beautifully designed, featuring tree-lined sidewalks, stunning architecture, and inviting storefronts. As you stroll, you'll notice the elegant buildings that house renowned brands, creating a visual feast that reflects Zurich's sophisticated atmosphere. The street is pedestrian-friendly, allowing visitors to take their time exploring the various shops and attractions.

Luxury Brands and Boutiques

Bahnhofstrasse is home to an impressive array of luxury brands and high-end boutiques. Here are some of the standout names that line this illustrious shopping street:

Louis Vuitton:
This iconic French fashion house is known for its luxury leather goods, fashion accessories, and ready-to-wear collections. The boutique on Bahnhofstrasse offers an extensive selection of the latest collections, as well as exclusive items available only in Zurich.

Chanel:
The Chanel boutique epitomizes elegance and sophistication. Shoppers can find a range of products, including classic handbags, fine jewelry, and haute couture. The boutique's luxurious interior design complements the brand's prestigious image.

Gucci:
Known for its bold designs and high-quality craftsmanship, the Gucci store offers a variety of luxury goods, including clothing, handbags, shoes, and accessories. The store often features seasonal collections and limited-edition items that attract fashion enthusiasts.

Hermès:
The Hermès boutique is famous for its timeless luxury goods, including the iconic Birkin and Kelly bags. The store also offers silk scarves, leather goods, and home accessories, all crafted with meticulous attention to detail.

Prada:

The Prada boutique showcases the brand's innovative designs and luxurious materials. Visitors can explore the latest collections of clothing, footwear, and accessories, all embodying the brand's avant-garde aesthetic.

Tiffany & Co.:
Renowned for its exquisite jewelry, Tiffany & Co. offers a stunning selection of engagement rings, necklaces, bracelets, and watches. The store's iconic blue boxes make it a popular destination for those seeking something special.

Burberry:
The Burberry store on Bahnhofstrasse features the brand's signature trench coats, stylish outerwear, and classic accessories. The store's modern design reflects Burberry's blend of heritage and contemporary fashion.

Bulgari:
Known for its bold and luxurious designs, Bulgari specializes in fine jewelry, watches, and accessories. The store offers unique pieces that often draw inspiration from Italian art and history.

Dolce & Gabbana:
The Dolce & Gabbana boutique features the brand's glamorous and eclectic style. Visitors can find everything from clothing and accessories to fragrances that embody Italian luxury and bold creativity.

Cartier:
The Cartier store is a destination for those seeking luxury watches and exquisite jewelry. Known for its craftsmanship and timeless elegance, Cartier offers a range of iconic pieces that reflect the brand's prestigious heritage.

Exclusive Shopping Experiences

Shopping on Bahnhofstrasse is not just about purchasing luxury items; it's also about the overall experience. Many boutiques offer personalized services, such as private shopping appointments, styling consultations, and bespoke products. Here are some of the exclusive shopping experiences available:

Personal Shopping:
Several luxury boutiques provide personal shoppers who assist clients in finding the perfect items tailored to their preferences. This service often includes private access to new collections and limited-edition pieces.

Exclusive Events:
Many high-end brands host exclusive events for their loyal customers, including private previews of new collections, trunk shows, and fashion shows. These events provide a unique opportunity to interact with designers and industry insiders.

Tailored Items:
Some boutiques offer bespoke services, allowing clients to customize products according to their specifications. Whether it's a personalized handbag or tailored clothing, these unique pieces become treasured possessions.

Culinary Experiences:
After a day of shopping, visitors can indulge in Zurich's culinary scene at one of the high-end cafés or restaurants along Bahnhofstrasse. Many luxury boutiques have adjacent cafés where shoppers can relax with a coffee or enjoy gourmet pastries, creating a well-rounded experience.

Cultural Touchpoints

In addition to luxury shopping, Bahnhofstrasse is also home to several cultural touchpoints that enhance the shopping experience:

Zurich's Paradeplatz:
This historic square, located at the intersection of Bahnhofstrasse and the city's financial district, is surrounded by impressive buildings and is a hub for both commerce and culture. It's also a great spot for people-watching and enjoying the atmosphere.

Historic Architecture:
The architecture along Bahnhofstrasse is a mix of modern and historic styles, with beautifully preserved buildings that tell the story of Zurich's development. Notable examples include the Hotel Baur Au Lac, a luxurious hotel that has hosted celebrities and dignitaries since 1844, and the Weltpostverein, known for its striking Art Nouveau design.

Public Art Installations:
Throughout Bahnhofstrasse, you can find various public art installations that add a contemporary flair to the traditional shopping experience. These artworks often reflect Zurich's artistic spirit and commitment to creativity.

Accessibility and Practical Tips

Bahnhofstrasse is easily accessible by public transport, with several tram and bus stops along the route. Visitors can take trams from Zurich Hauptbahnhof, which is just a short walk away from the beginning of the shopping district.

Best Times to Visit:
The best time to shop is during the weekday mornings when the street is less crowded. Weekends tend to be busier, especially during the holiday season when shops are decorated and offer special promotions.

Local Currency:
Switzerland uses the Swiss Franc (CHF). Most luxury boutiques accept major credit cards, but it's advisable to have some cash for smaller purchases or cafés.

Duty-Free Shopping:
International visitors may take advantage of duty-free shopping. Be sure to ask for a tax refund form when making purchases in eligible stores. This allows for a partial refund of the VAT upon leaving the country.

Bahnhofstrasse is a premier shopping destination that reflects Zurich's elegance and luxury. With its array of high-end boutiques and renowned international brands, the street offers a unique shopping experience that goes beyond mere consumerism. It's an opportunity to immerse oneself in a world of sophistication, artistry, and culture. Whether you're searching for a designer handbag, fine jewelry, or simply want to enjoy a leisurely day of window shopping and fine dining, Bahnhofstrasse invites you to experience the best of Zurich's high-end lifestyle.

Local Swiss Products To Look For

When shopping in Zurich, especially along Bahnhofstrasse, it's easy to get swept away by the allure of luxury brands and high-end boutiques. However, for those looking to take home a piece of Swiss culture, there are plenty of local products that showcase the country's craftsmanship, heritage, and flavors. Here are some must-try Swiss products to look for during your visit:

Swiss Watches

Switzerland is renowned for its watchmaking tradition, and no visit to Zurich would be complete without exploring the exquisite Swiss watches available for purchase. Look for brands that represent the pinnacle of horological craftsmanship:

Rolex:
A symbol of luxury and precision, Rolex watches are known for their timeless designs and impeccable performance.

Omega:
Famous for its connection to space exploration, Omega watches are a perfect blend of style and functionality.

TAG Heuer:
This brand is celebrated for its sports watches and chronographs, offering a modern aesthetic with Swiss precision.

Longines:

Known for elegance and tradition, Longines watches combine classic designs with reliable performance.

Many stores on Bahnhofstrasse offer not only the latest models but also vintage timepieces, allowing collectors to find unique additions to their collections.

Swiss Chocolates

Switzerland's reputation for chocolate is unmatched, and Bahnhofstrasse is home to several renowned chocolatiers. Here are some local favorites to look for:

Lindt:
Famous for its smooth chocolate and delectable truffles, Lindt offers a variety of products, including seasonal specialties.

Toblerone:
This iconic triangular chocolate bar is a classic Swiss treat that makes for a great souvenir.

Sprüngli:
Known for its luxurious pralines and the famous Luxemburgerli macarons, Sprüngli is a must-visit for chocolate lovers. The original Sprüngli café on Paradeplatz is a lovely spot to enjoy a sweet treat and a coffee.

Cailler:
As Switzerland's oldest chocolate brand, Cailler offers a range of artisanal chocolates made from traditional recipes. Look for their beautifully packaged chocolates for a unique gift.

Swiss Cheese

Switzerland is famous for its diverse cheese varieties, and many shops along Bahnhofstrasse offer the chance to purchase local cheeses. Some popular varieties include:

Emmental:
Known for its characteristic holes, Emmental cheese is mild and nutty, perfect for fondue or simply enjoying with bread.

Gruyère:
This hard cheese has a rich, slightly sweet flavor and is an essential ingredient in traditional Swiss fondue.

Raclette:
A semi-hard cheese that melts beautifully, Raclette is often used in the famous Swiss dish of the same name, where melted cheese is scraped onto boiled potatoes and pickles.

Appenzeller:
A flavorful cheese made in the Appenzell region, Appenzeller is known for its spicy and aromatic taste.

For cheese lovers, many shops offer sampling opportunities, allowing you to discover your favorites before purchasing.

Swiss Knives

The Swiss Army Knife is a versatile tool that has become an iconic symbol of Swiss ingenuity. Look for authentic Swiss Army Knives from Victorinox and Wenger, which come in various models with multiple functions, including blades, screwdrivers, scissors, and can openers. These handy tools make for practical souvenirs and are perfect for outdoor enthusiasts.

Traditional Swiss Souvenirs

In addition to luxury items, Bahnhofstrasse also offers various local souvenirs that reflect Swiss culture:

Cowbells:
These traditional bells are often decorated and make for charming decorative pieces or unique gifts.

Swiss Music Boxes:
Often featuring intricate designs and melodies, music boxes are a nostalgic reminder of Switzerland's cultural heritage.

Alpine Crafts:
Handmade wooden carvings, such as cuckoo clocks or figurines depicting Swiss folk traditions, can often be found in specialized shops.

Postcards and Art Prints:
Look for local artists' works or postcards featuring iconic Swiss landscapes and cityscapes to take home a piece of Zurich's beauty.

Local Wines and Spirits

Switzerland is home to various wine regions, and many local wines can be found in specialty shops. Consider trying:

Chasselas:
This white wine is the most widely grown grape in Switzerland, known for its light and fruity flavors. It pairs well with Swiss cheeses and fondue.

Pinot Noir:

This red wine, produced mainly in the Vaud and Valais regions, offers a range of flavors from berry notes to earthy undertones.

Grappa and Absinthe:
For those interested in spirits, look for Swiss grappa, a pomace brandy, or absinthe, a traditional Swiss herbal spirit known for its distinct flavor.

Swiss Fashion and Textiles

For unique fashion items, look for local Swiss designers that blend traditional craftsmanship with modern aesthetics:

Bally:
This luxury brand is known for its high-quality leather goods, shoes, and accessories, combining Swiss craftsmanship with contemporary design.

Akris:
A luxury fashion brand that offers elegant women's clothing made from the finest materials.

Mammut:
For outdoor enthusiasts, Mammut offers high-quality outdoor apparel and equipment designed for the Swiss Alps.

Shopping along Bahnhofstrasse in Zurich is not just about luxury brands; it's also an opportunity to discover and take home authentic Swiss products that reflect the country's rich culture and craftsmanship. From world-famous chocolates and artisanal cheeses to unique souvenirs and high-quality watches, Bahnhofstrasse offers a wide range of local delights for every visitor. Whether you're indulging in a piece of Swiss chocolate or investing in a luxurious timepiece, you're sure to find something that captures the essence of Switzerland during your visit.

Dining Along Bahnhofstrasse

As you explore Bahnhofstrasse, the excitement of luxury shopping is complemented by a delightful array of dining options that cater to various tastes and preferences. Whether you're in the mood for a quick coffee break, a leisurely lunch, or an elegant dinner, the street offers an impressive selection of cafés, restaurants, and bistros. Here are some notable dining options to consider while visiting Bahnhofstrasse:

Casual Cafés and Coffee Shops

For those looking to relax and recharge between shopping sprees, several cafés along Bahnhofstrasse provide a cozy atmosphere to enjoy a coffee or a light snack:

Café Sprüngli:
Located at Paradeplatz, this iconic café is a must-visit for its exquisite pastries, especially the famous Luxemburgerli macarons. You can enjoy a cup of coffee or hot chocolate while indulging in their delicious chocolate confections. The café's elegant interior and outdoor seating make it a perfect spot for people-watching.

Café Schober:
Situated just off Bahnhofstrasse in the picturesque Niederdorf district, Café Schober is known for its charming ambiance and delectable pastries. With an extensive menu featuring various coffee drinks, cakes, and traditional Swiss treats, it's an ideal place to unwind and savor the moment.

Kaffeekultur:

This specialty coffee shop focuses on high-quality brews and offers a selection of light bites, including sandwiches and pastries. The modern yet cozy atmosphere makes it a great spot for a quick coffee break.

Mid-Range Restaurants

If you're in the mood for a more substantial meal, several mid-range restaurants along Bahnhofstrasse provide a variety of culinary options, from Swiss classics to international cuisine:

Restaurant Swiss Chuchi:
Located in the heart of Zurich, this restaurant specializes in traditional Swiss dishes, including fondue and raclette. With a warm, rustic interior, it's a fantastic place to experience authentic Swiss cuisine.

Rive Gauche:
This stylish restaurant, situated within the Baur Au Lac hotel, offers a sophisticated dining experience with a menu that features Mediterranean-inspired dishes made from fresh, seasonal ingredients. The elegant ambiance and attentive service make it a perfect choice for a leisurely lunch or dinner.

Baltho Küche & Bar:
Combining contemporary design with a relaxed atmosphere, Baltho offers a seasonal menu inspired by international flavors. The restaurant emphasizes fresh, local ingredients and includes vegetarian and vegan options, making it an excellent choice for diverse dietary preferences.

Café de la Paix:
Located near the Opera House, this brasserie offers a blend of French and Swiss cuisine. With its beautiful terrace

overlooking the city, it's a lovely spot for lunch or dinner, featuring dishes like tartare and seasonal specialties.

Fine Dining Options

For those seeking a luxurious dining experience, Bahnhofstrasse and its surroundings are home to several high-end restaurants that promise an unforgettable culinary journey:

The Dolder Grand:
This five-star hotel features the acclaimed restaurant The Dolder Grand, which offers a Michelin-starred dining experience. The menu highlights creative European cuisine made with seasonal ingredients. The stunning views of Zurich and the Alps enhance the overall dining experience.

Pavillon:
Located in the Baur Au Lac hotel, Pavillon is another Michelin-starred restaurant that showcases exquisite French cuisine. The elegant setting, complete with a beautiful garden terrace, makes it a perfect venue for special occasions. The menu changes seasonally, highlighting the best local produce.

Zunfthaus zur Waag:
Situated in a historic guild house, this restaurant combines Swiss tradition with fine dining. The menu features gourmet interpretations of classic Swiss dishes, served in an opulent setting. It's an excellent choice for those looking to indulge in a refined dining experience.

Restaurant Kronenhalle:
A Zurich institution, this restaurant is famous not only for its gourmet cuisine but also for its impressive art collection

featuring works by artists like Chagall and Matisse. The menu offers a mix of Swiss and French dishes, and the elegant atmosphere makes it a favored spot for both locals and visitors.

International Cuisine

For those craving flavors from around the world, Bahnhofstrasse has several restaurants that offer international dishes, ensuring a diverse dining experience:

Café Azzurro:
This Italian café and restaurant serve a variety of pizzas, pastas, and authentic Italian dishes in a casual atmosphere. It's a great spot for a relaxed meal with friends or family.

Miki's Sushi:
For sushi lovers, Miki's offers a selection of fresh sushi and sashimi prepared with high-quality ingredients. The modern decor and vibrant atmosphere make it a popular choice for a light yet satisfying meal.

Tandoori:
If you're in the mood for Indian cuisine, Tandoori offers a delightful menu featuring traditional dishes such as curries, biryanis, and tandoori specialties. The warm ambiance and flavorful food provide a nice break from Swiss cuisine.

Dessert Spots

No dining experience is complete without dessert, and Bahnhofstrasse has plenty of options to satisfy your sweet tooth:

Confiserie Sprüngli:
In addition to its famous chocolates, Sprüngli offers a tempting selection of cakes, pastries, and desserts. Don't miss their signature Luxemburgerli macarons, available in various flavors.

Café Schober:
This café is also known for its delightful selection of desserts, including traditional Swiss pastries and cakes. Their Sachertorte and seasonal tarts are popular choices.

Gelato Shops:
If you're visiting during the warmer months, you'll find several gelato shops offering a variety of flavors made from fresh ingredients. These refreshing treats are perfect for a sweet pick-me-up while exploring the area.

Dining along Bahnhofstrasse is a delightful experience that complements the vibrant shopping scene. With a wide range of options from casual cafés to Michelin-starred restaurants, visitors can indulge in diverse culinary delights that showcase both local and international flavors. Whether you're stopping for a quick coffee, savoring Swiss specialties, or enjoying an elegant dinner, the dining scene along Bahnhofstrasse promises to satisfy every palate and create lasting memories during your visit to Zurich.

6

Activities On And Around Lake Zurich

Lake Zurich, with its stunning azure waters and breathtaking alpine backdrop, is one of the city's crown jewels and a major hub for outdoor activities and relaxation. The lake stretches approximately 40 kilometers (25 miles) along the Limmat River, offering a variety of recreational options for both locals and visitors. Here's a detailed look at the activities available on and around Lake Zurich, making it a perfect destination for nature lovers and adventure seekers.

Boating and Water Activities

One of the most enjoyable ways to experience Lake Zurich is from the water itself. There are several options for boating and water activities, catering to different preferences and interests:

Boat Cruises:
Several companies offer scenic boat cruises on Lake Zurich, allowing passengers to soak in the stunning views of the surrounding mountains and the charming lakeside villages. These cruises vary in duration and can range from short trips to longer excursions that may include a meal on board. The Zürichsee Verkehrs AG operates regular ferry services that

connect various towns around the lake, providing a unique perspective of the region while also serving as a convenient mode of transportation.

Sailing:
The calm waters of Lake Zurich make it an ideal location for sailing. You can either join a sailing school to learn the basics or rent a sailboat if you're already experienced. Several local clubs and companies offer boat rentals and organized sailing trips, where you can navigate the waters and enjoy the gentle breeze.

Stand-Up Paddleboarding (SUP):
For those looking for a fun and engaging way to explore the lake, stand-up paddleboarding has become increasingly popular. Rentals are available at various locations around the lake, and there are guided tours that offer instruction and take you to scenic spots.

Swimming:
In the summer months, swimming in Lake Zurich is a refreshing option. Several designated swimming areas, such as Utoquai and Zürichhorn, feature grassy banks and ladders for easy access to the water. The lake's temperature can rise to a pleasant 20–25 degrees Celsius (68–77 degrees Fahrenheit), making it inviting for a swim. There are also designated swimming zones with lifeguards on duty, ensuring safety for visitors.

Lakeside Parks and Beaches

The picturesque shoreline of Lake Zurich is lined with parks and beaches, offering idyllic settings for relaxation, picnics, and outdoor sports:

Zürichhorn Park:
This expansive park, located near the city center, features beautiful gardens, playgrounds, and walking paths. The lush green spaces provide a perfect spot for a picnic or a leisurely stroll along the lake. Visitors can also enjoy a meal at the Badi Zürichhorn, a lakeside restaurant with fantastic views.

Mythenquai:
This lakeside area boasts a popular public beach, making it an ideal destination for sunbathing and swimming. The sandy beach area is equipped with sun loungers, showers, and changing facilities, allowing visitors to fully enjoy a day by the water.

Rieterpark:
Located a short walk from the lake, Rieterpark is the largest park in Zurich and features sprawling lawns, historic villas, and the Museum Rietberg, which showcases non-European art. It's a beautiful spot for a peaceful walk or a picnic while enjoying the park's beautiful gardens.

Cycling and Walking Trails

For those who prefer to explore on foot or by bike, Lake Zurich offers numerous trails that wind around the shoreline, providing spectacular views and opportunities for outdoor exercise:

Lake Zurich Promenade:
The promenade stretches for several kilometers along the lake, providing a scenic path for walkers and joggers. The path is lined with trees, gardens, and benches, making it an inviting space for leisurely strolls or brisk walks.

Cycling Routes:
Biking around Lake Zurich is a popular activity, with dedicated cycling paths that allow you to enjoy the scenery while getting some exercise. You can rent bikes from various shops in the city or use the city's bike-sharing program. A popular cycling route is the 40-kilometer circuit around the lake, which can be completed in a few hours, depending on your pace.

Hiking Trails:
For a more adventurous experience, you can embark on one of the many hiking trails in the nearby hills and mountains that overlook Lake Zurich. The Uetliberg Mountain is a popular destination, offering panoramic views of the city and the lake. The hike to the summit takes about an hour from the base and is well worth the effort.

Winter Activities

While Lake Zurich is a summer paradise, it also offers a range of winter activities for those who enjoy the colder months:

Ice Skating:
In winter, parts of the lake may freeze over, creating opportunities for ice skating. While this is dependent on weather conditions, there are also several outdoor ice rinks in the city where you can enjoy skating regardless of lake conditions. Popular locations include Dolder Kunsteisbahn and Zürich Hauptbahnhof's temporary rinks during the holiday season.

Winter Hikes and Sledding:
The surrounding mountains become popular spots for winter hikes and sledding. There are various trails that can be

accessed from Zurich, providing beautiful snowy landscapes and family-friendly activities.

Lakeside Dining and Relaxation

After a day filled with outdoor adventures, relax at one of the many lakeside dining options:

Badi Utoquai:
A casual eatery located right on the lake, Badi Utoquai offers a variety of Swiss and international dishes, including fresh fish, salads, and refreshing beverages. The outdoor seating provides beautiful views of the lake and the surrounding mountains.

Restaurant Zürichhorn:
Nestled within Zürichhorn Park, this restaurant specializes in seasonal dishes made with fresh ingredients. With its beautiful terrace, it's an excellent spot to enjoy a meal while taking in the lake's serene ambiance.

Seebad Enge:
This unique venue features a swimming area and a restaurant where you can enjoy snacks and drinks. In the summer, the outdoor bar becomes a popular hangout spot, providing a lively atmosphere right by the water.

Festivals and Events

Lake Zurich hosts various festivals and events throughout the year, adding to its vibrant atmosphere:

Zürich Lake Festival:

Held every few years, this festival celebrates the beauty of Lake Zurich with boat parades, live music, cultural performances, and food stalls. It's a festive occasion that brings together locals and visitors for a memorable experience.

Fireworks on the Lake:
During special occasions, such as the Zürich Festival or national holidays, stunning fireworks displays light up the night sky over Lake Zurich. Watching the fireworks from the lakeside is a magical experience.

Lake Zurich is more than just a beautiful body of water; it's a hub for outdoor adventures and a serene escape from the hustle and bustle of city life. Whether you're boating, cycling, swimming, or simply enjoying a leisurely stroll along the promenade, the lake offers countless opportunities for relaxation and recreation. The surrounding parks and dining options make it an ideal spot for a day of exploration and enjoyment, allowing visitors to immerse themselves in the natural beauty and vibrant atmosphere of Zurich. Whether in summer or winter, Lake Zurich is a destination that promises to leave a lasting impression on anyone who visits.

Best Parks And Outdoor Spaces

Lake Zurich is not only renowned for its sparkling waters and scenic views but also for its abundance of parks and outdoor spaces that provide serene escapes, recreational activities, and opportunities to connect with nature. Here's a closer look at some of the best parks and outdoor spaces around Lake Zurich:

Zürichhorn Park

Located on the eastern shore of Lake Zurich, Zürichhorn Park is a beautifully landscaped area that offers a perfect mix of nature and relaxation. The park features:

Lush Gardens:
Visitors can stroll through well-maintained gardens filled with a variety of flowers, trees, and shrubs. The peaceful atmosphere makes it an ideal place for picnics or simply enjoying the beauty of nature.

Swimming Area:
The park includes a designated swimming area, known as Badi Zürichhorn, with facilities for sunbathing and swimming in the lake. It's a popular spot during the summer months, where families and friends gather to enjoy the sun and water.

Café and Restaurant:
The park is home to a lakeside café that serves refreshments and light meals, providing a lovely spot to take a break and soak in the views.
Cultural Events:

Throughout the year, Zürichhorn Park hosts various cultural events and festivals, adding vibrancy to the area and providing opportunities to engage with local traditions.

Utoquai

Utoquai is another picturesque park that stretches along the lakeside and offers stunning views of the water and surrounding mountains. Highlights include:

Promenade:
The promenade along Utoquai is perfect for leisurely walks, jogging, or cycling. The tree-lined path provides a pleasant atmosphere, making it popular with both locals and visitors.

Swimming Facilities:
This area is also known for its public swimming spots, where visitors can dive into the lake on warm days. The facilities include changing rooms and showers, ensuring a comfortable experience for swimmers.

Art Installations:
Utoquai features several sculptures and art installations along the lakeside, making it a lovely area for a stroll while appreciating art and nature.

Mythenquai

Mythenquai is a popular lakeside area known for its sandy beach and recreational facilities, making it a favorite destination for relaxation and fun:

Beach Area:

The sandy beach offers sun loungers, umbrellas, and shallow waters, making it perfect for families with children. It's an excellent spot for sunbathing or playing beach games.

Water Sports:
The area is popular for stand-up paddleboarding and kayaking. Equipment rentals are available nearby, providing an opportunity for visitors to engage in water sports.

Outdoor Restaurants:
Mythenquai has several outdoor dining options, allowing visitors to enjoy a meal or a drink with stunning views of Lake Zurich.

Rieterpark

Rieterpark is Zurich's largest park and offers a beautiful escape just a short distance from the lake. The park features:

Scenic Walking Paths:
The park's winding paths are perfect for leisurely walks, jogs, or cycling. The varied terrain includes hills, gardens, and shaded areas, creating a tranquil environment.

Museum Rietberg:
Within the park is the Museum Rietberg, which showcases a fascinating collection of non-European art. Visitors can explore the museum and then enjoy a peaceful stroll through the surrounding gardens.

Playgrounds and Picnic Areas:
Rieterpark is family-friendly, with several playgrounds and designated picnic areas where families can relax and enjoy the outdoors.

Arboretum

Located near the shores of Lake Zurich, the Arboretum is a botanical garden that showcases a diverse range of trees and plants from around the world. Highlights include:

Diverse Plant Species:
The Arboretum features over 1,500 different species of trees, shrubs, and plants, making it an educational and visually appealing destination for nature enthusiasts.

Walking Trails:
Well-maintained walking trails wind through the gardens, allowing visitors to explore at their own pace while enjoying the beauty of the flora.

Serene Atmosphere:
The peaceful environment of the Arboretum makes it an ideal place for reflection, relaxation, or even photography.

Lindenhof Hill

Lindenhof Hill is a historic park located in the city center, offering stunning views of the Old Town and Lake Zurich:

Historical Significance:
This park is situated on a former Roman castle site and holds great historical importance. Visitors can learn about its rich past while enjoying the serene atmosphere.

Scenic Views:
The hill provides panoramic views of the city and the lake, making it a popular spot for photos and relaxation.

Quiet Retreat:
Despite being centrally located, Lindenhof offers a quiet retreat from the bustling city, making it a lovely place to sit on a bench, read a book, or enjoy a moment of peace.

Hönggerberg

For those willing to venture a bit further, Hönggerberg offers beautiful hiking trails and stunning views of Zurich and the lake:

Hiking Trails:
Several well-marked trails wind through the hills, providing opportunities for hiking and nature walks. The terrain varies, catering to different fitness levels.

Picnic Spots:
The area features several picnic spots where visitors can enjoy a meal surrounded by nature. The scenic views make it a rewarding place to relax.

Panoramic Views:
From the higher points of Hönggerberg, visitors can enjoy breathtaking views of Lake Zurich, the city, and the distant mountains, particularly at sunset.

Greifensee

A short distance from Zurich, Greifensee is another beautiful lake that offers a tranquil environment and numerous outdoor activities:

Cycling and Walking Trails:

The lake is encircled by a scenic trail that is popular for cycling, jogging, and walking, providing a peaceful alternative to the busier Lake Zurich.

Bird Watching:
Greifensee is a nature reserve, making it an excellent spot for birdwatching, particularly during migration seasons. The lush surroundings are home to various bird species, providing a great opportunity for nature lovers.

Swimming and Picnicking:
There are designated swimming areas along the lake, along with parks and picnic spots for families to enjoy a day out.

The parks and outdoor spaces around Lake Zurich offer a rich tapestry of experiences for nature lovers, adventure seekers, and those simply looking to unwind. From bustling lakeside promenades to serene gardens and hiking trails, there is something for everyone to enjoy. Whether you're swimming, cycling, hiking, or relaxing in a park, the outdoor offerings in this beautiful city enhance the experience of visiting Lake Zurich, creating lasting memories of your time in Zurich.

Uetliberg Mountain: Hikes And Scenic Views

Uetliberg Mountain, affectionately known as Zurich's local mountain, is a cherished destination for residents and visitors alike. Standing at 871 meters (2,858 feet) above sea level, Uetliberg offers stunning panoramic vistas of Zurich, Lake Zurich, and the majestic Alps. This guide delves into the details of Uetliberg, covering how to get there, hiking opportunities, scenic views, dining options, and tour providers.

Getting to Uetliberg

Reaching Uetliberg is convenient and accessible:

Public Transport:
The easiest way to get to Uetliberg is by taking the Sihltalbahn (S-Bahn) train from Zurich's main station (Zürich Hauptbahnhof). The journey takes about 20 minutes to Uetliberg Station, where visitors can enjoy a short walk to the summit. Trains run frequently, typically every 30 minutes.

Hiking Trails:
For a more adventurous approach, several hiking trails lead to Uetliberg from various parts of Zurich. The trail from Triemli or Zürichberg provides a scenic and invigorating route for those looking to enjoy nature while hiking.

Hiking Opportunities

Uetliberg boasts an extensive network of well-marked hiking trails suitable for various skill levels:

Uetliberg Summit Trail:
This popular hike from Uetliberg Station to the summit is approximately 1 kilometer (0.6 miles) and takes about 30 minutes. The path is family-friendly and offers progressively breathtaking views as you ascend.

Planet Trail:
This unique 6-kilometer (3.7-mile) trail connects Uetliberg to Felsenegg and features stops representing the planets of our solar system. The hike takes about 1.5 to 2 hours and offers fantastic views of the city and lake along the way.

Zürich Mountain Trail:
For those seeking a longer adventure, the Zürich Mountain Trail stretches from Uetliberg to Wald and further to Küsnacht, covering around 11 kilometers (6.8 miles). This route combines picturesque landscapes and opportunities for hiking through diverse terrains.

Scenic Views and Photography

Uetliberg is celebrated for its spectacular views:

Observation Tower:
At the summit, visitors can climb the observation tower for an even higher vantage point. The climb up 87 steps rewards hikers with a 360-degree view of Zurich, Lake Zurich, and, on clear days, the stunning Swiss Alps. This spot is particularly popular for photographers, especially during sunrise or sunset.

Photo Opportunities:

Numerous lookout points along the trails and at the summit provide excellent opportunities for capturing the beauty of the city and lake. The vibrant scenery is perfect for stunning photographs.

Wildlife and Nature

The Uetliberg region is a haven for nature lovers:

Flora and Fauna:
The area is rich in biodiversity, with various plant species and wildlife. Hikers might spot deer, foxes, and numerous bird species as they traverse the trails. The diverse ecosystems allow for close-up observations of local flora and fauna.

Seasons:
Uetliberg transforms with the seasons, providing different experiences year-round. Spring brings blooming wildflowers, summer offers lush greenery, autumn showcases vibrant foliage, and winter turns the area into a snowy wonderland, ideal for winter hiking and snowshoeing.

Dining and Relaxation

After a day of hiking, there are great dining options at Uetliberg:

Uto Kulm Restaurant:
Located near the summit, this restaurant offers a cozy atmosphere and stunning views of Zurich and the lake. Guests can enjoy Swiss cuisine, including hearty local dishes and seasonal specialties. Prices at Uto Kulm typically range from CHF 25 to CHF 45 for main courses, making it a delightful place to unwind after a hike.

Picnicking:
Many scenic spots along the trails and at the summit are perfect for picnicking. Bring your own snacks or meals to enjoy in the fresh air surrounded by nature.

Tour Providers and Charges

For those who prefer a guided experience, several tour providers offer excursions to Uetliberg, each with varying costs and services:

Zurich Hiking Tours:
This company offers guided hikes to Uetliberg, including a tour of the Planet Trail. Prices typically range from CHF 50 to CHF 80 per person, depending on the length and inclusions of the tour. They provide knowledgeable guides who share insights about the flora, fauna, and history of the area.

Swiss Travel System:
For those looking to combine transportation and a guided experience, the Swiss Travel System offers packages that include train tickets and guided tours. Prices vary but generally start at CHF 100 per person for a half-day tour, including a train ticket from Zurich.

Alpine Adventures:
Specializing in outdoor experiences, Alpine Adventures offers tailored hiking tours to Uetliberg. Prices for private tours begin at CHF 150 per person, which includes a personal guide and customized itineraries.

Airbnb Experiences:

Local guides often list Uetliberg hikes on platforms like Airbnb Experiences, where prices can range from CHF 40 to CHF 90 per person for group hikes, often including snacks and drinks.

Events and Activities

Uetliberg also hosts various events and activities throughout the year:

Guided Tours:
During the warmer months, guided hiking tours are available, led by locals who share insights about the ecology and history of the area. These tours provide a deeper understanding of the region's culture and natural beauty.

Winter Sports:
In winter, Uetliberg becomes a popular destination for snowshoeing and winter hiking. Local organizations often offer guided snowshoe tours, allowing visitors to explore the snow-covered landscape.

Uetliberg Mountain is a treasure trove of natural beauty, outdoor adventure, and breathtaking views, making it an essential stop for anyone visiting Zurich. Whether you hike to the summit for the stunning panoramas, explore the network of trails, or simply relax in the lush surroundings, Uetliberg provides a unique escape into nature without straying far from the city. With its accessible location, diverse range of activities, and the option of guided tours, Uetliberg is the perfect destination for outdoor enthusiasts, families, and anyone looking to enjoy the beauty of Zurich's natural landscape.

7

Traditional Swiss Dishes: Fondue, Raclette, And More

Zurich's culinary scene is a delightful blend of tradition and modernity, showcasing the best of Swiss cuisine. The city offers a variety of dining options, from cozy bistros to upscale restaurants, where visitors can savor iconic Swiss dishes. Here, we delve into the traditional flavors of Zurich, focusing on beloved classics such as fondue, raclette, and other local specialties.

Fondue: A Swiss Classic

Fondue is perhaps the most iconic Swiss dish, known for its communal dining experience and rich flavors. It originated in the alpine regions of Switzerland and has become a staple in Zurich and throughout the country.

What is Fondue?
Fondue consists of melted cheese, typically a mix of Gruyère and Emmental, blended with white wine, garlic, and a splash of kirsch (cherry brandy). The mixture is heated in a special pot, called a caquelon, and served with long forks and pieces of crusty bread for dipping. As diners gather around the pot,

the experience is as much about the food as it is about the social interaction.

Where to Enjoy Fondue in Zurich:
Several restaurants in Zurich specialize in fondue, creating an authentic Swiss dining experience:

- **Swiss Chuchi**: Located in the heart of the Old Town, this restaurant is famous for its traditional fondue, served in a cozy, rustic setting. Prices typically range from CHF 30 to CHF 45 per person, depending on the cheese selection.

- **Le Dezaley**: This charming restaurant offers a selection of fondues, including variations like truffle or mushroom fondue. Prices are similar to Swiss Chuchi, and the atmosphere reflects traditional Swiss hospitality.

- Chäs-Mägg: This small, intimate eatery specializes in cheese dishes, including fondue and raclette. Their fondue is particularly well-reviewed, with prices around CHF 28 per person.

Raclette: The Cheesy Delight

Raclette is another beloved Swiss dish that revolves around melted cheese but differs from fondue in presentation and preparation.

What is Raclette?
Raclette cheese, a semi-hard variety, is melted and scraped off the wheel onto boiled potatoes, pickles, and cured meats. The cheese is traditionally melted using a special grill or a raclette

machine, making it a fun and interactive dining experience. This dish is particularly popular during the winter months, providing a hearty meal that warms the soul.

Where to Enjoy Raclette in Zurich:
Several places in Zurich serve this delicious dish:

- **Raclette Stube**: This restaurant is dedicated to raclette and offers a range of options, from classic to innovative twists. Diners can enjoy the interactive process of melting cheese at their table. Prices usually range from CHF 35 to CHF 50 per person, depending on the selection.

- **Restaurant Zeughauskeller**: Located in a historic building, this restaurant serves traditional Swiss cuisine, including raclette. The lively atmosphere and hearty portions make it a popular choice, with prices around CHF 32 per person.

Zürcher Geschnetzeltes: A Local Specialty

While fondue and raclette are the stars of Swiss cuisine, Zurich has its own traditional dish: Zürcher Geschnetzeltes.

What is Zürcher Geschnetzeltes?
Zürcher Geschnetzeltes is a creamy veal dish sautéed with mushrooms and served in a white wine and cream sauce. It's typically accompanied by Rösti, a Swiss potato dish that is crispy on the outside and soft on the inside. This dish captures the essence of Zurich's culinary heritage.

Where to Enjoy Zürcher Geschnetzeltes in Zürich:
Several restaurants offer this local favorite:

- **Restaurant Zunfthaus zur Waag**: A traditional eatery known for its Zürcher Geschnetzeltes, served in a historic setting. Prices are around CHF 38 to CHF 50 per serving.

- **Haus Hiltl**: As the world's oldest vegetarian restaurant, Haus Hiltl offers a vegetarian version of Zürcher Geschnetzeltes, made with mushrooms and tofu. Prices range from CHF 28 to CHF 40.

Other Traditional Swiss Dishes

Beyond fondue, raclette, and Zürcher Geschnetzeltes, Zurich's culinary landscape features several other traditional dishes worth exploring:

Rösti:
A quintessential Swiss dish, Rösti is made from grated potatoes that are pan-fried until crispy. It can be served as a side dish or topped with ingredients like cheese, eggs, or smoked salmon. Many restaurants, including Kronenhalle, serve a delicious version.

Älplermagronen:
This hearty Alpine dish combines pasta, potatoes, cheese, and cream, often topped with fried onions. It's a comforting meal perfect for colder months and is available at restaurants like Alpenrose.

Saffron Risotto:
Though not traditionally Swiss, saffron risotto has gained popularity in Zurich due to its Italian influences. This creamy dish is often found on the menus of upscale restaurants like Giesserei and is typically priced between CHF 30 and CHF 50.

Dessert Delights

No culinary journey in Zurich would be complete without indulging in Swiss desserts:

Chocolate:
Switzerland is world-renowned for its chocolate, and Zurich is home to numerous chocolatiers. Confiserie Sprüngli is famous for its Luxemburgerli macaroons and pralines, while Läderach offers exquisite chocolate creations. Prices for chocolates vary, but a box of pralines typically starts at CHF 20.

Rösti Cake:
A delightful dessert variation of the savory Rösti, this cake features layers of potatoes, apples, and cinnamon. It's a unique treat found in local bakeries and cafés.

Torta di Noci:
A walnut cake that is often served with whipped cream, this dessert is a staple in Swiss pastry shops and makes for a perfect end to a meal.

Wine and Beverages

Pairing traditional dishes with local beverages enhances the dining experience:

Swiss Wines:
Switzerland produces excellent wines, especially whites like Chasselas. Many restaurants offer local wines that pair beautifully with Swiss dishes. Expect to pay around CHF 8 to CHF 15 for a glass of Swiss wine.

Appenzeller:

A regional herbal liqueur, Appenzeller is often served as an aperitif or after a meal. It has a distinctive flavor profile and is worth trying for its unique taste.

Dining Experiences in Zurich

Zurich's culinary scene is not just about the food; it's also about the experience. Here are a few unique dining options:

Food Tours:
Consider joining a food tour to discover the culinary delights of Zurich. Companies like "Food Zurich" offer guided tours where you can sample traditional dishes, visit local markets, and learn about the city's culinary history. Prices typically range from CHF 90 to CHF 130 per person.

Cooking Classes:
For those interested in learning how to prepare Swiss dishes, cooking classes are available. Local chefs offer classes on making fondue or traditional pastries. Prices for classes usually start at CHF 100 per person.

Zurich's culinary scene is a reflection of its rich cultural heritage and modern influences. With traditional dishes like fondue, raclette, and Zürcher Geschnetzeltes, as well as an array of delightful desserts, visitors are in for a treat. The city offers a vibrant dining experience, from cozy local eateries to upscale restaurants, making it a destination for food lovers. Embrace the flavors of Switzerland and immerse yourself in the warmth and hospitality that Zurich's culinary scene has to offer.

Best Restaurants, Bistros, And Food Markets

Zurich's culinary landscape is rich and diverse, offering a variety of dining options that cater to all tastes and budgets. From fine dining establishments to charming bistros and bustling food markets, Zurich is a gastronomic paradise. Here's a closer look at some of the best places to eat and experience the local food culture.

Best Restaurants

Zurich is home to a number of renowned restaurants that showcase both traditional Swiss dishes and innovative cuisine:

Restaurant ETH Zurich:
Located within the ETH Zurich University, this restaurant boasts breathtaking views of the city and Lake Zurich. The menu features a mix of Swiss and international dishes, with an emphasis on fresh, seasonal ingredients. Prices range from CHF 30 to CHF 60 for main courses.

Restaurant Kronenhalle:
This iconic Zurich establishment is famous for its classic Swiss dishes and its stunning art collection, featuring works by famous artists like Chagall and Picasso. The menu offers traditional favorites like Zürcher Geschnetzeltes and homemade desserts. Main courses typically cost between CHF 40 and CHF 70.

Baur Au Lac:

One of Zurich's most prestigious hotels, Baur Au Lac features a fine dining restaurant that focuses on seasonal, locally sourced ingredients. The Michelin-starred restaurant serves contemporary cuisine with a touch of elegance. Expect to pay around CHF 80 to CHF 200 for a multi-course meal.

Charming Bistros

For a more casual dining experience, Zurich has numerous bistros and brasseries where visitors can enjoy hearty meals in a relaxed setting:

Café Anvers:
This charming café is known for its cozy atmosphere and delicious brunch offerings, including Swiss specialties and fresh pastries. It's an ideal spot to enjoy a leisurely meal. Prices range from CHF 15 to CHF 25 for brunch dishes.

Café Noir:
A popular neighborhood bistro, Café Noir serves a mix of Swiss and Mediterranean dishes, including fresh salads, pasta, and homemade desserts. The casual ambiance makes it a great spot for a laid-back dinner, with prices typically between CHF 20 and CHF 35 for main courses.

Bistro Le Dezaley:
Located near the central train station, this bistro specializes in traditional Swiss cuisine, particularly fondue and raclette. The friendly staff and rustic decor create a warm atmosphere. Prices for fondue start at CHF 28 per person.

Food Markets

Exploring Zurich's food markets is a fantastic way to experience local culture and taste a variety of foods. Here are some of the best markets to visit:

Zurich Street Food Festival:
This lively festival, held several times a year, brings together food trucks and vendors from around the city, offering a diverse array of international cuisines and local specialties. Admission is usually free, with dishes priced between CHF 5 and CHF 15, making it an affordable way to sample different flavors.

Markthalle im Viadukt:
Located under the railway viaduct, this indoor market features a variety of food stalls and shops selling fresh produce, meats, cheeses, and baked goods. It's an excellent spot to grab a quick bite or pick up local ingredients. Enjoy casual dining at one of the market's small eateries, where prices for a meal typically range from CHF 15 to CHF 25.

Helena Frey Markt:
This traditional market, held weekly, offers an array of local products, including fruits, vegetables, cheese, and artisanal goods. It's a great place to experience Zurich's local food culture and engage with local vendors.

Oerlikon Market:
Held every Tuesday and Friday, this vibrant market features a wide selection of fresh produce, flowers, and local delicacies. It's perfect for picking up ingredients for a picnic or enjoying street food from local vendors.

Unique Dining Experiences

For those looking for something a bit different, Zurich offers several unique dining experiences:

Dinner in the Sky:
This extraordinary dining event allows guests to enjoy a meal suspended high above the city. With breathtaking views and a gourmet menu prepared by top chefs, it's a once-in-a-lifetime experience. Prices typically start at CHF 250 per person for a multi-course meal.

Fondue Tram:
For a truly unique experience, hop aboard the Fondue Tram, where guests can enjoy a delicious cheese fondue while touring the city's scenic streets. The ride typically lasts about two hours, and prices are around CHF 85 per person, including the fondue.

Cooking Classes:
Participate in a cooking class to learn how to make traditional Swiss dishes, such as fondue and Rösti. Local chefs offer hands-on classes that allow participants to enjoy their creations afterward. Prices usually start at CHF 100 per person.

Zurich's culinary scene is a delightful mix of traditional Swiss cuisine and modern culinary influences. With a range of restaurants, charming bistros, and vibrant food markets, visitors can experience the best of what the city has to offer. Whether you're indulging in a classic fondue, exploring local specialties at a market, or enjoying a unique dining experience, Zurich's food culture promises to leave a lasting impression. So come hungry and prepare to savor the flavors of this beautiful Swiss city.

Vegetarian And Vegan Options

As Zurich continues to embrace diverse culinary trends, the city has become increasingly accommodating to vegetarians and vegans. With a growing number of restaurants, bistros, and cafés offering plant-based options, Zurich provides a vibrant dining scene that caters to those seeking delicious and sustainable meals. Here's a comprehensive look at the vegetarian and vegan options available in the city.

Vegetarian and Vegan Restaurants

Several restaurants in Zurich specialize in vegetarian and vegan cuisine, showcasing innovative dishes made with fresh, local ingredients:

Hiltl:
Recognized as the world's oldest vegetarian restaurant, Hiltl has been serving delicious plant-based meals since 1898. The extensive buffet features a wide range of options, from salads and curries to homemade pastries. Diners can choose from an all-you-can-eat buffet or order from an à la carte menu. Prices typically range from CHF 30 to CHF 45 for a meal.

Tibits:
This popular chain offers a vibrant buffet of vegetarian and vegan dishes inspired by international flavors. With a focus on seasonal ingredients, Tibits allows diners to create their own plates and pay by weight. Expect to spend around CHF 20 to CHF 35 for a hearty meal. The relaxed atmosphere makes it an excellent spot for lunch or dinner.
Vegan Junk Food:

Located in Zurich's trendy district, this casual eatery serves a variety of indulgent vegan fast food, including burgers, fries, and milkshakes. The menu is designed to cater to those seeking comfort food without compromising on taste. Prices range from CHF 15 to CHF 25 for a meal, making it an affordable option for a satisfying meal on the go.

Cafés and Bakeries with Plant-Based Options

In addition to dedicated vegetarian and vegan restaurants, many cafés and bakeries in Zurich offer plant-based options for breakfast and snacks:

Café Baltho:
This cozy café features a selection of vegetarian and vegan breakfast options, including smoothie bowls, avocado toast, and freshly baked pastries. The inviting atmosphere makes it a great place to relax with a cup of coffee. Prices for breakfast items typically range from CHF 10 to CHF 20.

Café Zuckerman:
Known for its delicious vegan pastries and cakes, Café Zuckerman is a must-visit for those with a sweet tooth. The café offers a range of plant-based treats, including cupcakes and tarts, perfect for an afternoon snack. Prices for pastries generally range from CHF 4 to CHF 8.

Kaffeekeller:
This quaint coffee shop is a haven for vegans, serving plant-based coffees, teas, and light snacks. Their vegan cakes and pastries are popular among locals, and the relaxed atmosphere makes it a perfect spot for a casual meet-up. Expect to pay around CHF 3 to CHF 7 for drinks and snacks.
Supermarkets

Zurich's supermarkets and food markets also cater to vegetarian and vegan diets, offering a wide selection of plant-based products:

Coop and Migros:
These major supermarket chains offer extensive vegetarian and vegan sections, featuring everything from plant-based meats and dairy alternatives to frozen meals and snacks. Shoppers can find a variety of products, including vegan cheeses, soy-based yogurts, and meat substitutes. Prices vary but generally range from CHF 3 to CHF 15, depending on the product.

Food Festivals and Events

Zurich hosts several food festivals that celebrate plant-based cuisine, providing opportunities to explore vegetarian and vegan dishes from various cultures:

Zurich Vegan Festival:
This annual event brings together local vegan businesses, food trucks, and restaurants, offering a wide variety of plant-based dishes. Attendees can sample everything from savory meals to sweet treats, and the festival often features cooking demonstrations and workshops. Admission is usually free, with prices for food items ranging from CHF 5 to CHF 15.

Food Zurich:
This city-wide food festival showcases Zurich's culinary diversity, including many events focused on vegetarian and vegan cuisine. Visitors can participate in special tastings, cooking classes, and themed dinners, with prices varying based on the event.

Grocery Stores and Specialty Shops

For those interested in cooking at home, Zurich offers several grocery stores and specialty shops with a focus on vegetarian and vegan ingredients:

Bioladen:
This organic grocery store specializes in natural and organic products, including a variety of vegetarian and vegan options. From fresh produce to specialty items like vegan cheeses and plant-based meats, shoppers can find everything they need for healthy cooking. Prices typically range from CHF 3 to CHF 20, depending on the product.

Vegibund:
A specialty shop dedicated to vegetarian and vegan products, Vegibund offers a range of plant-based foods, including snacks, condiments, and pantry staples. The knowledgeable staff can help shoppers find the best products to suit their dietary needs. Prices vary but are generally affordable.

Zurich's culinary scene is increasingly accommodating to vegetarian and vegan diets, offering a plethora of delicious options for those seeking plant-based meals. With a mix of dedicated vegetarian restaurants, cafés with vegan treats, and supermarkets stocking a variety of plant-based products, there is no shortage of choices. Whether you're indulging in a hearty meal at Hiltl, enjoying a sweet pastry at Café Zuckerman, or exploring local markets, Zurich invites you to savor its vibrant food culture while embracing a more sustainable lifestyle. The city's commitment to diversity in cuisine ensures that everyone can find something delightful to enjoy.

8

Live Music And Cultural Events

Zurich boasts an eclectic nightlife scene that ranges from sophisticated lounges and rooftop bars to bustling live music venues and hidden underground clubs. Whether you're looking to relax with a craft cocktail, dance to live tunes, or experience Zurich's cultural events after dark, the city offers a vibrant mix of options for locals and visitors alike. Here's a guide to some of Zurich's best spots for nightlife and live entertainment.

Trendy Bars and Lounges

Zurich is home to an array of stylish bars and lounges that attract a lively crowd. Here are some of the most popular spots for an unforgettable night out:

Widder Bar:
Located in Zurich's Old Town, Widder Bar is famous for its impressive selection of whiskies and signature cocktails crafted by expert mixologists. The stylish decor and live jazz performances create an elegant atmosphere. Cocktails typically cost between CHF 18 and CHF 25.

Clouds:

Situated on the 35th floor of the Prime Tower, Clouds is a sophisticated bar offering breathtaking views of Zurich's skyline. Known for its well-curated wine and cocktail menu, it's a popular spot for a romantic night out or an upscale gathering with friends. Prices for drinks start at around CHF 15.

Kronenhalle Bar:
An iconic Zurich establishment, Kronenhalle Bar is a must-visit for its classic cocktails and impressive art collection, featuring works by artists like Picasso and Chagall. The timeless ambiance makes it a favorite for both locals and tourists. Cocktails are priced between CHF 20 and CHF 30.

Frau Gerolds Garten:
This unique, bohemian-style garden bar offers a relaxed setting with eclectic decor and outdoor seating. Located near the Viadukt shopping area, it's a perfect place to enjoy a casual evening with friends, especially during Zurich's warmer months. Beers and cocktails typically cost CHF 10 to CHF 15.

Hiltl Dachterrasse:
Part of the world's oldest vegetarian restaurant, the Hiltl rooftop bar offers a cozy setting with an extensive menu of drinks, vegetarian bites, and lively events. With its indoor and outdoor areas, Hiltl Dachterrasse is ideal for an evening out with views over Bahnhofstrasse. Expect drink prices around CHF 12 to CHF 18.

Live Music and Cultural Events

Zurich's live music scene caters to a range of tastes, from jazz and classical performances to contemporary rock, indie, and electronic music. The city hosts several renowned music festivals and offers a variety of live music venues:

Moods:
Located in the Schiffbau area, Moods is one of Zurich's premier jazz clubs, known for hosting a range of genres including jazz, soul, funk, and electronic music. With performances by both local and international artists, Moods provides an intimate atmosphere perfect for music lovers. Tickets generally cost between CHF 20 and CHF 50, depending on the artist.

Kaufleuten:
Kaufleuten is a legendary Zurich venue that combines a nightclub, concert hall, and restaurant all under one roof. Known for its eclectic lineup of events, including live music performances, DJ sets, and cultural evenings, Kaufleuten is a must-visit spot for Zurich's nightlife. Ticket prices for live events vary, usually starting at CHF 30.

Tonhalle Zurich:
For a more classical music experience, Tonhalle Zurich hosts performances by the Tonhalle Orchestra, as well as visiting symphonies and soloists. Located near Lake Zurich, the elegant concert hall attracts classical music enthusiasts from around the world. Ticket prices for concerts typically range from CHF 40 to CHF 150.

Opera House Zurich (Opernhaus Zürich):
Zurich's Opera House is one of Europe's most respected venues, offering a year-round calendar of opera, ballet, and orchestral performances. The beautiful neoclassical building is worth a visit, even if just for a tour. Tickets for performances

can range from CHF 30 to over CHF 200, depending on the show.

Mascotte:
One of Zurich's oldest clubs, Mascotte hosts live music events, comedy shows, and DJ nights, making it a popular destination for a lively evening. With a diverse lineup that includes everything from indie bands to electronic music, Mascotte is an essential stop for nightlife enthusiasts. Tickets are usually priced between CHF 15 and CHF 40.

Unique Nightlife Experiences and Festivals

Zurich also offers some unique nightlife experiences and cultural festivals that make the city's evening scene truly stand out:

Street Parade:
One of the largest techno parades in the world, Zurich's Street Parade attracts hundreds of thousands of visitors every August. The open-air event features international DJs, live performances, and colorful floats parading along the shores of Lake Zurich. Admission is free, though some after-parties require tickets.

Zurich Openair:
This popular music festival, held in late summer, showcases a mix of international and local acts, spanning genres like indie, rock, hip-hop, and electronic music. Zurich Openair attracts a young, vibrant crowd and includes both daytime and nighttime performances. Ticket prices start around CHF 100 for a day pass.

Rote Fabrik:

Located on the shores of Lake Zurich, Rote Fabrik is a cultural center housed in a former factory building. It hosts a variety of events, including live music, theater performances, art exhibitions, and open-air movies. Many events are low-cost or free, with live music tickets generally priced between CHF 10 and CHF 30.

Zurich's nightlife scene is as diverse as the city itself, offering a wealth of options that cater to different tastes and styles. From elegant cocktail lounges and rooftop bars with stunning views to bustling live music venues and high-energy clubs, Zurich promises a memorable night out for every type of visitor. With a mix of traditional and contemporary venues, and an ever-evolving calendar of events, Zurich's nightlife is an integral part of the city's vibrant cultural fabric, offering locals and tourists alike a chance to experience the city in a whole new light.

Nightclubs And Zurich's Nightlife Districts

Zurich's nightlife districts each offer distinct vibes and a range of nightclubs for late-night fun. While Zurich may be known for its serene lake and historic charm, it also boasts a robust nightlife scene that surprises visitors with an eclectic mix of clubs, live music venues, and social spaces that stay open well into the early hours. For those looking to experience Zurich's after-hours pulse, here's a guide to its most popular nightlife areas and clubs.

Langstrasse: Zurich's Bohemian Heart

Langstrasse, Zurich's most famous nightlife district, is a vibrant and multicultural area where eclectic energy meets endless nightlife possibilities. Known for its unconventional charm, Langstrasse is home to a mix of bars, restaurants, live music venues, and clubs. From grungy dive bars to sophisticated cocktail lounges, Langstrasse offers a diverse experience for every taste.

-Club Zukunft:
One of the city's best electronic music clubs, Zukunft is beloved by locals for its underground vibe and excellent DJ lineups, featuring techno, house, and experimental sounds. The club has an intimate setting, with a focus on immersive music experiences rather than flashy decor. Entrance fees usually range from CHF 15 to CHF 25.

Klaus:
A stylish and minimalist club, Klaus attracts a slightly older crowd looking for an upscale but relaxed night out. Known for

its carefully curated playlists and intimate dance floor, it's a perfect spot for those who enjoy house and deep techno music without the big-club vibe. Entry fees are generally around CHF 10 to CHF 20.

Gonzo Club:
Gonzo is a small but lively venue offering alternative music, live gigs, and occasional hip-hop nights. The club's grunge-inspired atmosphere, casual vibe, and late-night hours make it popular among Zurich's younger crowd. Entry fees range from CHF 10 to CHF 15.

Langstrasse itself is an attraction, with colorful street art, buzzing bars, and an unpretentious feel. The area's clubs are complemented by numerous late-night food spots where revelers can grab a quick snack before heading home.

Zurich-West: Industrial Chic and Urban Innovation

Zurich-West, an area transformed from industrial warehouses into trendy hangouts, offers a vibrant nightlife scene with some of Zurich's best clubs and unique venues. Known for its modern architecture and hip aesthetic, Zurich-West attracts a trendy crowd and is ideal for those seeking a mix of high-energy dance floors and chill social spots.

Hive:
A must-visit for electronic music enthusiasts, Hive features a spacious dance floor, top-notch sound system, and a consistent lineup of local and international DJs. Hive's industrial setting and stylish lighting create a captivating atmosphere, making it a favorite among techno and house music fans. Entry fees typically range from CHF 20 to CHF 35.

Supermarket:
This Zurich-West mainstay is known for its minimalist design and exceptional lineup of techno and electronic acts. Supermarket attracts a mixed crowd of both Zurich locals and visitors and is particularly popular on weekends when it hosts top DJs from around the world. Entry fees are around CHF 20.

Frau Gerolds Garten:
While technically more of a beer garden than a nightclub, Frau Gerolds Garten in Zurich-West is a lively outdoor spot that offers an excellent pre-party atmosphere with drinks, food, and casual music. In the winter, the venue transforms with cozy igloos, making it a unique seasonal experience.

Zurich-West's nightlife is characterized by its innovative spaces, with clubs often housed in repurposed factories and warehouses. The area's industrial charm gives it a distinct urban edge, setting it apart from other parts of Zurich.

Niederdorf: Old Town Charm Meets Contemporary Vibes

Niederdorf, located in Zurich's historic Old Town, combines old-world charm with modern nightlife options. Known for its narrow streets, medieval buildings, and lively cafés, Niederdorf becomes a bustling nightlife area in the evenings, with an array of clubs and bars that cater to different tastes.

Plaza Klub:
Located in a historic building, Plaza Klub is one of Zurich's most popular spots, offering themed parties, DJ nights, and live music. The club attracts a diverse crowd and features multiple rooms, each with a distinct style. It's a versatile

venue, often featuring genres like pop, R&B, and electronic. Entry fees range from CHF 15 to CHF 30.

Mascotte:
As one of Zurich's oldest clubs, Mascotte has a rich history of hosting live music and dance nights. Known for its vibrant ambiance, the club offers a variety of events, including international indie bands, hip-hop nights, and DJ sets. Mascotte's central location in Niederdorf makes it a convenient choice for travelers. Entry fees are usually CHF 20 to CHF 35.

Oliver Twist Pub:
Although not a nightclub in the traditional sense, Oliver Twist is a lively British-style pub that has been part of Niederdorf's nightlife for decades. Known for its casual atmosphere and live sports screenings, it's a great spot to start the night before heading to nearby clubs.

Niederdorf is ideal for a more laid-back night out, as it features a mix of energetic clubs and quaint pubs, making it suitable for those looking to experience Zurich's historic center with a modern twist.

Seefeld: Upscale and Relaxed Nightlife

Seefeld, located along Lake Zurich, is known for its upscale bars and lounges, offering a more refined nightlife experience. This district is perfect for visitors looking to unwind with a cocktail while enjoying scenic lake views. The nightlife in Seefeld leans towards the sophisticated side, appealing to an older crowd or those who prefer an elegant setting.

Rimini Bar:

Located along the Sihl river, Rimini Bar is an outdoor bar that turns into a laid-back nightlife spot during the warmer months. With its beach-like vibe and relaxed setting, Rimini Bar is ideal for a casual evening with friends. The entrance is free, and drinks are moderately priced, making it a popular choice for warm summer nights.

Sablier Rooftop Bar:
This rooftop bar offers breathtaking views of Zurich and an extensive cocktail menu. Known for its chic ambiance, Sablier provides a mix of live DJ performances and lounge music, creating an atmosphere that's sophisticated yet relaxed. Drinks here are on the pricier side, with cocktails starting at around CHF 18.

La Stanza:
A classy cocktail bar known for its high-quality drinks and cozy atmosphere, La Stanza attracts a stylish crowd. Its intimate setting makes it ideal for a quieter night out or a romantic evening with a partner. Cocktails range from CHF 15 to CHF 25.

Seefeld's nightlife offers an alternative to the bustling club scenes of Langstrasse and Zurich-West, providing a quieter, more elegant experience for those who prefer sipping cocktails in a serene atmosphere by the lake.

Practical Tips for Navigating Zurich's Nightlife

Transportation:
Zurich's public transportation system runs frequently during the day, but night services are limited. Trams and buses operate on a night schedule during weekends, with night buses covering major areas between 1:00 a.m. and 4:00 a.m.

Taxi services are also available, though fares are higher at night.

Dress Code:
Zurich clubs tend to have a smart-casual dress code, particularly in upscale areas like Seefeld. It's best to avoid overly casual attire, especially when visiting high-end bars or lounges.

Entry Fees and Age Restrictions:
Most clubs charge entry fees, generally between CHF 10 and CHF 35, depending on the venue and event. The legal drinking age in Zurich is 18 for beer and wine and 20 for spirits, so be prepared to show ID at the door.

Zurich's nightlife districts each offer their own unique flavor, from the gritty and eclectic Langstrasse to the upscale and chic Seefeld. Whether you're seeking a night of dancing, enjoying live music, or simply unwinding with a cocktail by the lake, Zurich's diverse nightlife has something for everyone, making the city a lively and memorable destination long after the sun goes down.

9

Exploring The Swiss Alps

For visitors in Zurich, the Swiss Alps are within easy reach and offer some of the most stunning natural landscapes in the world. Known for their rugged peaks, pristine lakes, and charming mountain villages, the Alps provide an ideal escape from city life. While an overnight stay is ideal for fully immersing in the Alpine environment, several areas are reachable as day trips from Zurich, offering breathtaking views and exhilarating outdoor experiences. Here's a detailed look at some of the best ways to explore the Swiss Alps on a day trip from Zurich.

Jungfrau Region: The "Top of Europe"

The Jungfrau Region, one of the most iconic Alpine destinations, is home to the famous Jungfraujoch railway station, dubbed the "Top of Europe" due to its high altitude and panoramic views. Jungfraujoch sits at an elevation of 3,454 meters (11,332 feet) and is accessible by an unforgettable train journey. From Zurich, you can reach the Jungfrau Region within about 2-3 hours by train, making it a feasible day trip.

Getting There:

Take a train from Zurich HB (main station) to Interlaken, where you transfer to the Jungfraujoch railway. It's recommended to purchase tickets in advance, especially during the high season. The round-trip train journey costs approximately CHF 200-240 per person, though discounts are available with Swiss Travel Pass and other railcards.

Highlights:
The trip to Jungfraujoch is an adventure in itself, featuring a cogwheel train ride through stunning mountain scenery, including stops at scenic lookout points. Once at the top, you'll have access to the Ice Palace, Sphinx Observatory, and the Snow Fun Park, where visitors can try skiing, snowboarding, and sledding year-round.

Best Time to Visit:
The Jungfrau Region is stunning throughout the year, but summer (June to September) offers clear skies and accessible trails for hiking, while winter (December to March) is ideal for skiing and snowboarding.

Mount Titlis: Eternal Snow and Breathtaking Views

Mount Titlis, located near the village of Engelberg, is another excellent day-trip destination from Zurich. Known for its eternal snow and glaciers, Titlis offers visitors an Alpine adventure year-round. The Titlis Rotair, the world's first rotating cable car, provides panoramic views of the mountain landscape on the way to the summit.

Getting There:
From Zurich HB, take a train to Engelberg, where you'll find a cable car station for the ascent to Mount Titlis. The journey

takes around 1.5 to 2 hours one way. A round-trip ticket for the cable car to the summit costs about CHF 96 per person.

Highlights:
Mount Titlis offers a range of activities, including the famous Titlis Cliff Walk, Europe's highest suspension bridge, and Glacier Cave, where you can walk through tunnels of ice. In winter, Titlis is a popular spot for skiing and snowboarding. During summer, visitors can hike the trails, try the Glacier Park snow tubing, or simply enjoy the scenery from the viewing platforms.

Best Time to Visit:
Mount Titlis is accessible year-round. Winter offers ideal conditions for snow sports, while summer is perfect for hiking and the Cliff Walk.

Lucerne and Mount Pilatus: An Iconic Mountain and Medieval Town

Lucerne, just an hour from Zurich, combines the charm of a historic Swiss town with the stunning views of nearby Mount Pilatus. Visitors can enjoy the medieval architecture of Lucerne before ascending to Pilatus, which offers some of the best panoramic views in the Alps.

Getting There:
Trains from Zurich to Lucerne run frequently and take about an hour. To reach Mount Pilatus, take a cogwheel train from Alpnachstad (available from May to November) or a cable car from Kriens (open year-round). A round-trip ticket for the Mount Pilatus Golden Round Trip costs around CHF 72-92 per person.

Highlights:
The journey up Pilatus on the cogwheel train is a thrilling experience, as the railway is one of the steepest in the world. At the top, visitors can enjoy panoramic views of Lake Lucerne and the surrounding mountains, dine at one of the mountaintop restaurants, or hike along the ridge trails.

Best Time to Visit:
Mount Pilatus is ideal to visit in the summer (June to September) for the most stable weather, though it can be visited in winter by cable car. However, winter visitors should check for any closures before planning their trip.

Rigi Mountain: The "Queen of the Mountains"

Mount Rigi, known as the "Queen of the Mountains," is an accessible and beautiful destination offering stunning views of Lake Lucerne and the Alps. With a network of trails and viewpoints, Rigi is popular for hiking and relaxation.

Getting There:
From Zurich, take a train to Arth-Goldau, where you can board the cogwheel train up to Rigi Kulm. The journey takes around 1.5 hours from Zurich. The Rigi Round Trip ticket costs about CHF 72 per person, with discounts available for Swiss Travel Pass holders.

Highlights:
Visitors can enjoy scenic hikes, relax at the mineral baths, or take in the view from Rigi Kulm, the highest peak. For those looking for an easy-going excursion, Rigi offers shorter, less strenuous trails than other Alpine destinations. In winter, Rigi is also popular for snowshoeing and winter walking.

Best Time to Visit:
Rigi is accessible year-round, with winter offering scenic snowy landscapes and summer featuring lush green meadows.

Schilthorn: The James Bond Mountain

Schilthorn is known for its appearance in the James Bond movie "On Her Majesty's Secret Service". Located in the Bernese Oberland region, it offers impressive views of the Eiger, Mönch, and Jungfrau mountains and is an exciting destination for movie buffs and nature lovers alike.

Getting There:
From Zurich, take a train to Lauterbrunnen and then a series of cable cars to the summit. The round-trip fare from Lauterbrunnen to Schilthorn costs about CHF 105 per person.

Highlights:
At the summit, visitors can enjoy the Piz Gloria revolving restaurant, the James Bond exhibit, and the 007 Walk of Fame, an outdoor display of photos and facts about the iconic film. The Thrill Walk, a glass-bottom walkway along the cliffs, offers a unique adrenaline rush.

Best Time to Visit:
Schilthorn can be visited year-round, but clear weather in summer (June to September) is best for unobstructed views.

Grindelwald and First: Alpine Adventure and Hiking Paradise

Grindelwald, a charming mountain village, serves as a gateway to incredible hiking trails and adventures around

Mount First. Known for its pristine trails, Grindelwald offers everything from leisurely walks to intense hikes.

Getting There:
From Zurich, take a train to Grindelwald (around 2 hours). The cable car ride from Grindelwald to First costs approximately CHF 64 for a round-trip ticket.

Highlights:
From the top of First, you can explore the First Cliff Walk, an exhilarating steel walkway overhanging the cliffs, or take part in the First Flyer zip line. In summer, hiking trails leading to Lake Bachalpsee offer one of Switzerland's most iconic views.

Best Time to Visit:
Summer (June to September) is ideal for hiking and outdoor activities, while winter transforms the area into a snowy playground for skiers and snowboarders.

Tips for Day Tripping to the Alps from Zurich

Early Start:
Plan to leave Zurich early to maximize your time in the mountains, as many of these journeys require at least 1-2 hours of travel.

Swiss Travel Pass:
Consider purchasing a Swiss Travel Pass, which covers many trains, buses, and cable cars at a discounted rate, making it cost-effective for day trips.

Weather Check:

Mountain weather can change quickly. Check the forecast before heading out, especially if planning outdoor activities like hiking or skiing.

Dress in Layers:
Temperatures in the Alps can vary significantly throughout the day. Dress in layers to stay comfortable.

Each of these Alpine destinations offers a unique perspective on Switzerland's natural beauty, cultural heritage, and adventure opportunities. Whether you're looking for breathtaking views, exciting activities, or a serene escape from the city, these Swiss Alps day trips provide an unforgettable extension of your Zurich experience.

Rhine Falls And Surrounding Towns

Just a short distance from Zurich lies the magnificent Rhine Falls, Europe's largest waterfall. Located near the town of Schaffhausen, the falls are a must-see for anyone visiting Zurich. The area around Rhine Falls is steeped in history and offers picturesque towns, vineyards, and castles, making it an ideal day trip for those looking to experience Switzerland's natural beauty and historic charm.

Rhine Falls: A Natural Wonder

The Rhine Falls, spanning 150 meters (490 feet) across and plunging 23 meters (75 feet) over a jagged cliff, offers an awe-inspiring sight and a thrilling experience. Formed during the last Ice Age, the falls have attracted visitors for centuries with their thunderous roar and stunning appearance.

Getting There:
Rhine Falls is easily accessible from Zurich. A direct train from Zurich HB (main station) to Schloss Laufen am Rheinfall station takes around 45 minutes. Alternatively, buses and guided tours provide convenient options for reaching the falls.

Highlights:
Visitors can walk right up to the falls via viewing platforms that get close enough to feel the mist. Boat tours allow guests to approach the falls from the water, providing a unique angle and closer experience. A round-trip boat ride costs approximately CHF 20, with additional fees if you opt to climb the famous rock that stands at the center of the falls.
Best Time to Visit:

Summer (June to September) is an ideal time, as the snowmelt and rainfall cause the Rhine to swell, enhancing the volume and intensity of the falls. Visiting during late spring or early fall offers a quieter experience with fewer tourists, while winter presents a tranquil, frozen landscape for a unique view of the falls.

Exploring Schloss Laufen: The Rhine Falls Castle

Perched above the Rhine Falls is Schloss Laufen, a medieval castle that provides a stunning vantage point over the falls and offers visitors an opportunity to step back in time. Dating back to the 9th century, this historic castle has been carefully preserved, with museum exhibits, scenic walkways, and cultural insights that add depth to a visit.

Getting There:
Schloss Laufen is accessible from the train station of the same name, just a short walk away. Visitors can enter the castle grounds and enjoy views from terraces overlooking the falls.

Highlights:
Inside the castle, there's a small museum showcasing the history and formation of the falls, as well as artifacts from the region's history. The viewing terrace offers panoramic views of the Rhine River and the falls below, making it an excellent spot for photography.

Admission Fees:
Entry to the viewing platforms at Schloss Laufen costs around CHF 5 per person, with discounts available for students, children, and groups.

The Town of Schaffhausen: A Medieval Gem

Just a few kilometers from Rhine Falls, Schaffhausen is a charming medieval town that transports visitors to another era. Known for its well-preserved medieval architecture, colorful frescoed buildings, and cobbled streets, Schaffhausen offers a relaxing contrast to the dynamic experience at the falls.

Getting There:
Schaffhausen is a quick 10-minute train ride from Schloss Laufen. Trains run frequently between Zurich and Schaffhausen, making it easy to add a visit to the town as part of your day trip.

Highlights:
Schaffhausen's Old Town is full of historical landmarks, including the Munot Fortress, a 16th-century circular fort that provides panoramic views of the surrounding area. Stroll along Vordergasse, the main street, lined with ornate guild houses, cafes, and boutiques. Don't miss the Museum zu Allerheiligen, which showcases regional archaeology, art, and history, housed within a former monastery.

Stein am Rhein: Switzerland's Most Picturesque Town

A little further from Rhine Falls, Stein am Rhein is one of Switzerland's most beautiful towns, famous for its meticulously preserved half-timbered houses and vibrant frescoes. This small medieval town sits along the banks of the Rhine River and is perfect for a relaxing exploration of Swiss history, culture, and natural beauty.

Getting There:

From Zurich, you can reach Stein am Rhein by train in about an hour. A popular route is to take a boat along the Rhine from Schaffhausen, which offers scenic views of vineyards, small villages, and the serene river landscape.

Highlights:
Stein am Rhein's central square, Rathausplatz, is lined with colorfully frescoed buildings and offers a fairy-tale atmosphere. Key landmarks include the Hohenklingen Castle, which dates back to the 13th century and provides views over the town and river. For those interested in history, the St. George's Abbey Museum offers insights into the town's medieval roots.

Boat Trips Along the Rhine River

The Rhine River offers scenic boat tours that allow visitors to enjoy the peaceful beauty of the river valley. Several operators provide tours between Schaffhausen, Stein am Rhein, and other riverside towns, making it possible to explore the region at a relaxed pace.

Boat Tour Options:
Boat cruises are available from Schaffhausen to Stein am Rhein, lasting around 90 minutes one way. Tickets for a single ride are approximately CHF 15, and round-trip options are available. Some operators offer multi-stop tickets, allowing passengers to disembark and explore multiple locations along the Rhine before reboarding.

Wine Tasting in the Blauburgunderland Region

The region surrounding the Rhine River near Schaffhausen is known as Blauburgunderland, or "Pinot Noir Country," due to its abundant vineyards. Here, visitors can enjoy wine-tasting experiences at local wineries, with a particular focus on Pinot Noir and other regional wines. Many wineries offer tours and tastings that can be paired with local cheeses and cured meats.

Getting There:
From Schaffhausen, visitors can take local buses or guided wine tours that provide transportation to several nearby wineries.

Highlights:
Visit traditional family-owned wineries and taste some of the best Swiss wines, which are less commonly available outside Switzerland. Popular wineries like GVS Schaffhausen and Weingut Besson-Strasser offer informative tours that delve into the wine-making process, the history of local vineyards, and the unique characteristics of Swiss wines.

Tour Costs:
Wine-tasting experiences vary but typically start around CHF 20-30 per person, depending on the number of wines and any additional offerings such as cheese or charcuterie.

Planning Your Day Trip to Rhine Falls and Surrounding Towns

When visiting Rhine Falls, consider combining it with a stop in Schaffhausen and, if time allows, an afternoon in Stein am Rhein. This combination allows you to experience the natural beauty of the falls, the historical richness of Schaffhausen, and the storybook charm of Stein am Rhein.

Early Start:

Begin your journey early to ensure ample time at each destination, especially if you plan to visit multiple towns.

Swiss Travel Pass:
Consider purchasing a Swiss Travel Pass, as it often covers the train and boat routes mentioned, making travel convenient and cost-effective.

Weather Considerations:
Check the weather before departing, especially for outdoor activities near the falls and river.

Dining Options:
There are several cafes and restaurants near Rhine Falls, Schaffhausen, and Stein am Rhein, offering traditional Swiss fare. Be sure to try local dishes like Rösti, raclette, and fresh fish from the Rhine River.

Exploring Rhine Falls and the surrounding towns allows travelers to witness Switzerland's multifaceted beauty—from dramatic waterfalls to tranquil riverside towns, from medieval architecture to renowned vineyards. This trip perfectly complements a visit to Zurich and gives a taste of Swiss history, culture, and natural wonders.

Other Nearby Destinations: Lucerne, Basel, and More

Zurich's central location in Switzerland makes it a prime starting point for day trips to some of the country's most scenic and culturally rich destinations. While Rhine Falls and the surrounding towns offer a mix of natural beauty and medieval charm, nearby cities like Lucerne and Basel present an array of historical, cultural, and scenic experiences. Here's a closer look at a few nearby destinations that make for perfect day trips from Zurich.

Lucerne: Lake Views and Mountain Adventures

Nestled on the shores of Lake Lucerne, with views of towering mountains like Mount Pilatus and Mount Rigi, Lucerne is a city that effortlessly combines natural beauty with a rich history. Known for its well-preserved medieval architecture, waterfront promenades, and vibrant arts scene, Lucerne is one of Switzerland's top tourist destinations.

Getting There:
Lucerne is about a 45-minute train ride from Zurich, with frequent connections throughout the day, making it an easy day trip.

Highlights:
A visit to Lucerne often begins with the Chapel Bridge (Kapellbrücke), a charming wooden bridge adorned with colorful flowers and historic paintings. Nearby, the Old Town (Altstadt) is filled with frescoed buildings, boutique shops,

and cafes. For art and culture enthusiasts, the Rosengart Collection features works by Picasso and other modern masters.

Lake Lucerne Cruises:
A scenic cruise on Lake Lucerne offers spectacular views of the surrounding mountains and quaint villages. There are several cruise options, ranging from short trips to longer excursions, including meals and narrated guides. Tickets start around CHF 30, with premium options available.

Mountain Excursions:
Lucerne is also the gateway to famous mountain excursions, such as the steep cogwheel railway up Mount Pilatus or the cable car ride to Mount Rigi. These trips provide stunning panoramic views and opportunities for hiking or simply enjoying the alpine scenery. Prices for these excursions vary but generally start at around CHF 70.

Basel: Switzerland's Cultural Capital

Located near the borders of France and Germany, Basel is renowned for its vibrant arts scene, historical architecture, and annual art fairs that attract enthusiasts from around the globe. As Switzerland's cultural capital, Basel is an intriguing blend of medieval and modern, with a rich tapestry of museums, galleries, and a cosmopolitan atmosphere.

Getting There:
Basel is about an hour away from Zurich by train, with regular service throughout the day.

Highlights:

The Old Town of Basel is home to the red sandstone Basel Minster, a Gothic cathedral dating back to the 12th century. Visitors can explore the Rathaus (Town Hall) with its distinctive red façade and colorful murals. Basel is also known for its diverse range of museums, such as the Kunstmuseum (Fine Arts Museum), Fondation Beyeler, and the Tinguely Museum, dedicated to the kinetic artist Jean Tinguely.

Art and Culture:
Basel hosts Art Basel each year, one of the world's premier modern art fairs, drawing collectors, artists, and curators from around the world. Even outside the event, the city's art galleries and theaters, like the Basel Theatre, offer a variety of cultural events.

River Cruises:
Basel is situated along the Rhine River, and river cruises are a popular way to enjoy the city from a different perspective. Boat trips along the Rhine offer scenic views and occasionally cross the border into neighboring Germany and France. Cruise prices range from CHF 20-50 depending on the length and amenities.

Winterthur: Switzerland's Hidden Gem of Art and Industry

Located just 20 minutes by train from Zurich, Winterthur may not be as well-known as Lucerne or Basel, but it has a rich industrial history and is now a hub for art and technology. The city is home to several excellent museums, beautiful parks, and a charming Old Town.

Highlights:

The Old Town of Winterthur is one of Switzerland's largest pedestrian zones, with cozy cafes, shops, and historic buildings. Winterthur's Fotomuseum and Kunstmuseum house impressive photography and art collections, while Technorama, the Swiss Science Center, offers interactive exhibits for all ages.

Nature and Parks:
Winterthur is known for its green spaces, such as the Eulachpark and Rosengarten, which are perfect for a relaxed stroll or picnic. The Eschenberg Forest nearby offers hiking trails and an observatory for stargazing enthusiasts.

Appenzell: Traditional Swiss Culture and Alpine Scenery

Appenzell is a charming town known for its distinct Swiss traditions, colorful houses, and stunning alpine landscapes. Located in the eastern part of Switzerland, the area around Appenzell is popular for hiking, cheese tasting, and experiencing authentic Swiss culture.

Getting There:
Appenzell is about an hour and a half from Zurich by train, with a change in Gossau.

Highlights:
The town itself is quaint and picturesque, with its brightly painted wooden buildings and traditional Swiss architecture. Visitors can explore the Appenzell Museum to learn about local history, customs, and folklore. A visit wouldn't be complete without sampling Appenzeller cheese, known for its distinct flavor. Many farms and dairies in the region offer cheese-tasting experiences.

Alpine Hiking:
Appenzell is also a gateway to some of Switzerland's best hiking routes. The Ebenalp mountain offers scenic trails, caves, and the famous Aescher cliffside restaurant. The hike to Aescher takes about an hour from the top of the Ebenalp cable car and rewards visitors with breathtaking views.

Rapperswil: The Town of Roses

Rapperswil, located on the shores of Lake Zurich, is a picturesque medieval town known as the "Town of Roses" for its lovely rose gardens and scenic lakeside location. Its historic charm, beautiful lakeside promenade, and views of the Alps make it a delightful escape from Zurich.

Getting There:
Rapperswil is about a 30-minute train ride from Zurich. Alternatively, a boat ride from Zurich to Rapperswil along Lake Zurich takes about two hours and provides beautiful scenery along the way.

Highlights:
Visitors to Rapperswil can wander through the Old Town, visit Rapperswil Castle, and explore the rose gardens, which bloom in spring and summer. The town's wooden bridge, the Holzbrücke Rapperswil-Hurden, connects Rapperswil with the nearby village of Hurden and is one of the oldest wooden footbridges in Europe.

Lakeside Activities:
The lakeside area in Rapperswil is perfect for picnicking, swimming, or renting a paddleboat to enjoy Lake Zurich. The Knies Kinderzoo, a small but charming zoo founded by

Switzerland's Knie Circus family, is a favorite for families with children.

From historic towns to awe-inspiring landscapes, Zurich's surrounding regions offer visitors a wealth of experiences, each showcasing a unique aspect of Swiss culture, natural beauty, and tradition. Whether it's a lakeside lunch in Lucerne, a river cruise in Basel, or a scenic hike near Appenzell, these day trips allow travelers to experience Switzerland's diversity, all within easy reach of Zurich.

10

Zürifäscht, Zurich Film Festival, And Street Parade

Zurich's festivals and seasonal events add layers of excitement and cultural richness to the city throughout the year. From massive music gatherings and colorful parades to cultural celebrations and film festivals, Zurich's calendar is filled with events that cater to a diverse array of interests. Here's a closer look at some of the city's most renowned festivals, including Zürifäscht, Zurich Film Festival, and Street Parade.

Zürifäscht: Zurich's Largest City Festival

Zürifäscht, held every three years, is the largest public festival in Zurich, drawing over two million visitors from Switzerland and beyond. Celebrated during the first weekend of July, Zürifäscht transforms Zurich's lakeside and city center into a massive open-air festival filled with attractions, food stalls, music stages, and fireworks.

History:
Zürifäscht began as a traditional celebration in Zurich, symbolizing the city's love for community gatherings, music, and fun. Over the years, it has grown into a highly anticipated

event, attracting international visitors. The last Zürifäscht was held in 2023, and the next one is scheduled for 2026.

Activities and Attractions:
The festival features everything from fairground rides and street performances to food stalls offering Swiss and international cuisine. Adventure-seekers can enjoy carnival-style rides, bungee jumping, and water activities on Lake Zurich. The Sechseläutenplatz, Bellevue, and Bürkliplatz are some of the festival's main locations, bustling with various shows and performances.

Fireworks Display:
A highlight of Zürifäscht is its spectacular fireworks, lighting up the Zurich skyline twice during the festival weekend. The synchronized music and colorful explosions attract massive crowds along the lakefront. For those looking for a premium view, boat cruises on Lake Zurich offer an exclusive vantage point, with tickets available for purchase ahead of the festival.

Food and Drink:
Stalls offering traditional Swiss delicacies like raclette, bratwurst, and Swiss pastries line the streets. Additionally, visitors can enjoy international cuisine, craft beers, cocktails, and wines, making it a food lover's paradise. Prices at the food stalls range from CHF 5-20 depending on the type of dish.

Zürifäscht is an experience for all ages, blending local culture, music, and entertainment into one unforgettable weekend. It's wise to book accommodations and dining reservations in advance, as the city is particularly busy during this celebration.

Zurich Film Festival (ZFF): Celebrating International Cinema

The Zurich Film Festival, held annually in September and October, is Switzerland's most significant film event, showcasing an impressive lineup of national and international films, documentaries, and short films. Known for its unique blend of glamor and intimate screenings, ZFF attracts filmmakers, actors, and cinephiles from around the world.

History and Purpose:
Founded in 2005, the Zurich Film Festival quickly established itself as a platform for emerging filmmakers and a showcase for innovative cinema. It has become one of Europe's most respected film festivals, emphasizing cultural exchange and providing networking opportunities within the film industry.

Festival Highlights:
The Zurich Film Festival spans about 11 days and includes premieres, panel discussions, and workshops. Each year, the festival features films from various genres, ranging from drama and comedy to thriller and documentary. Categories include "Focus," highlighting Swiss, German, and Austrian films, and "International Feature," which showcases films from around the globe.

Venues:
Screenings take place at various iconic locations in Zurich, including the Corso Cinema, the Arthouse Le Paris, and the Filmpodium. Each venue is selected to provide an intimate setting, allowing audiences to engage closely with the films and filmmakers.

Special Guests and Awards:

The festival has attracted a roster of international stars and directors over the years, such as Cate Blanchett, Johnny Depp, and Hugh Jackman. The Golden Eye Awards are presented to outstanding films and filmmakers, covering categories such as Best International Film, Best Documentary, and Best Emerging Director.

Tickets:
Tickets for the Zurich Film Festival typically range from CHF 20-30 per screening, with discounts available for students and festival pass holders. Early booking is recommended, especially for premieres and events featuring high-profile guests.

ZFF is an incredible opportunity for film enthusiasts to discover new cinematic talents, attend premieres, and experience Zurich's vibrant cultural scene.

Street Parade: Europe's Largest Techno Parade

Street Parade, held annually on the second Saturday of August, is Zurich's answer to Berlin's Love Parade and has grown to become the largest techno parade in Europe. This electrifying event celebrates electronic dance music (EDM) and attracts hundreds of thousands of people who gather around Lake Zurich to dance, party, and experience the unique energy of this iconic parade.

Origins and Growth:
The first Street Parade took place in 1992, initiated by student Marek Krynski as a small demonstration for peace, love, and techno music. Since then, it has become one of the world's largest and most famous electronic music parades, drawing DJs and fans from across the globe.

The Route:
Street Parade follows a 2.4-kilometer route along the lake, starting at Utoquai and ending near the Hafen Enge. Around 30 "Love Mobiles"—colorful, DJ-equipped trucks blasting music—move slowly along the route, surrounded by dancing crowds and onlookers.

Music and DJs:
Some of the biggest names in the electronic music world, including Carl Cox, David Guetta, and Armin van Buuren, have performed at Street Parade. The event also features local and up-and-coming DJs, offering a mix of electronic genres such as house, techno, and trance. Multiple stages are set up along the lake, each offering a different electronic music experience.

Atmosphere and Dress Code:
Street Parade is known for its vibrant, inclusive atmosphere, where attendees of all ages express themselves through colorful outfits, costumes, and body paint. The dress code is casual, and participants are encouraged to get creative with their attire.

Safety and Tips:
With hundreds of thousands of people attending, it's essential to stay hydrated, wear comfortable shoes, and protect valuables. Zurich's public transport system runs extended hours during Street Parade, allowing attendees to move safely around the city.

Street Parade is not just a festival; it's a massive, high-energy gathering that brings together people from different cultures and backgrounds, united by a love for music, dance, and freedom.

Additional Seasonal Events in Zurich

Beyond these three signature festivals, Zurich hosts several other seasonal events that add charm and variety to the city's cultural landscape.

Sechseläuten:
Held every April, this traditional spring festival involves the burning of the "Böögg," a snowman effigy, symbolizing the end of winter. The festival includes a parade of Zurich's guilds, colorful costumes, and music. The burning of the Böögg is accompanied by much excitement, as locals believe the quicker it burns, the warmer the summer will be.

Christmas Markets:
Zurich transforms into a winter wonderland during the holiday season, with Christmas markets filling the city. The market at Zurich Hauptbahnhof is the largest indoor Christmas market in Europe, featuring a massive Swarovski-decorated Christmas tree. Smaller markets around the city, like those at Sechseläutenplatz and Niederdorf, offer mulled wine, Swiss treats, and handmade gifts.

Knabenschiessen:
This traditional Zurich festival takes place in September and is centered around a historic shooting competition for Swiss boys and girls. Although the focus is on the competition, the festival also features rides, food stalls, and live music, making it a popular family event.

Zurich Openair:
For fans of contemporary music, Zurich Openair, held in late August, brings international and Swiss bands to Zurich for a four-day outdoor festival featuring indie, pop, and electronic

acts. Tickets range from CHF 100-200 for day passes, with weekend passes also available.

New Year's Eve Fireworks:
Each New Year's Eve, Zurich hosts a spectacular fireworks show over Lake Zurich, organized by the Zurich Hoteliers' Association. This event draws large crowds who gather along the lakefront to welcome the new year with music, food stalls, and a midnight firework display.

Zurich's festivals and seasonal events reflect the city's dynamic spirit, blending Swiss traditions with global influences. From lively techno parades and elegant film festivals to traditional guild parades and cozy Christmas markets, there's something to experience in every season. These events not only offer entertainment but also provide insight into Zurich's culture, fostering a sense of community and celebration that resonates with locals and visitors alike.

Winter Attractions: Christmas Markets And Activities

Zurich truly comes alive during the winter season, transforming into a festive wonderland that delights both locals and visitors. With sparkling Christmas markets, enchanting holiday lights, and seasonal activities, winter in Zurich offers an experience that's as magical as it is memorable. Here's a look at Zurich's top winter attractions, from bustling Christmas markets to cozy seasonal traditions.

Christmas Markets: A Zurich Winter Tradition

Zurich's Christmas markets are among the most famous in Switzerland, attracting people who come to enjoy the warm, festive atmosphere and indulge in Swiss seasonal specialties. Each market has its own unique character, with beautiful decorations, handcrafted goods, and traditional treats.

Christkindlimarkt at Zurich Hauptbahnhof:
Located in Zurich's main train station, the Christkindlimarkt is one of Europe's largest indoor Christmas markets. The focal point here is the towering 15-meter-tall Christmas tree adorned with over 7,000 Swarovski crystals, casting a sparkling glow across the market. The market offers more than 140 stalls, featuring everything from handmade gifts and Swiss chocolates to mulled wine and festive pastries. This market is ideal for those looking to escape the cold while browsing a broad selection of gifts and treats.
Operating Dates: Typically runs from mid-November until Christmas Eve.

Wienachtsdorf at Sechseläutenplatz:
Set near the beautiful Opera House, this open-air market feels like a cozy Christmas village with wooden chalets, twinkling lights, and festive decorations. Wienachtsdorf is known for its artisanal crafts, local jewelry, and unique gifts, making it a popular spot for gift shopping. Visitors can also indulge in Swiss favorites like raclette and fondue, as well as international foods from various vendors. The market also features an ice rink where both adults and children can skate while soaking in the holiday spirit.
Operating Dates: Runs from late November to December 23.

Dörfli Christmas Market in Niederdorf:
Zurich's oldest Christmas market, located in the charming Old Town district of Niederdorf, is known for its romantic, historic ambiance. The market's narrow, winding lanes are lined with stalls selling handcrafted ornaments, cozy winter accessories, and regional foods. Dörfli Christmas Market is perfect for a relaxed stroll through the medieval streets, with vendors offering mulled wine, roasted chestnuts, and Swiss pastries that fill the air with holiday aromas.
Operating Dates: Generally held from late November until Christmas Eve.

Each Christmas market provides a unique experience, inviting visitors to explore Zurich's festive side, sample Swiss delicacies, and find one-of-a-kind holiday gifts.

Ice Skating and Winter Sports

Zurich has several ice rinks and winter sports options that add an active element to the winter experience. Whether it's an outdoor rink in the heart of the city or a quick trip to a nearby mountain for skiing, there are plenty of ways to embrace the winter season.

Ice Skating at Wienachtsdorf (Sechseläutenplatz):
The open-air rink at the Wienachtsdorf Christmas Market is a popular choice for ice skating enthusiasts, especially families. Set against the backdrop of the Opera House, it's both scenic and convenient, with rentals available on-site.

Dolder Ice Rink:
Located on the hills above Zurich, the Dolder Ice Rink (Dolder Kunsteisbahn) is one of the largest open-air ice rinks in Europe. The rink offers stunning views of the city and the lake and is surrounded by nature, providing a peaceful setting to enjoy winter sports. Skates can be rented on-site, and there's even a small café serving hot chocolate and snacks to warm up after skating.
Entrance Fees: Approximately CHF 8 for adults and CHF 6 for children, with skate rentals available for around CHF 7.

Skiing and Snowboarding Near Zurich:
While Zurich itself doesn't have ski slopes, several ski resorts are located within an hour's drive or train ride, making it easy for visitors to enjoy Switzerland's famous alpine activities. Some popular nearby resorts include:

- Flumserberg: Located about an hour's drive from Zurich, Flumserberg is one of the most accessible ski resorts from the city, offering slopes for all skill levels. A day pass typically costs around CHF 60-70 for adults.
- Hoch-Ybrig: Another convenient choice near Zurich, Hoch-Ybrig offers a variety of slopes, snow parks, and panoramic views. It's an ideal destination for both

beginner and intermediate skiers, with day passes costing about CHF 45-50.

- Engelberg-Titlis: A bit further away but highly popular, Engelberg-Titlis is known for its well-maintained slopes and stunning scenery. Tickets range around CHF 70 for a day pass, with frequent public transport options connecting Zurich and Engelberg.

Fondue and Raclette Experiences

Winter in Zurich wouldn't be complete without indulging in Swiss fondue and raclette, two beloved winter dishes that provide warmth and comfort. Many restaurants in Zurich offer traditional Swiss dining experiences centered around melted cheese.

Fondue Tram:
For a unique twist on a classic meal, the Fondue Tram offers a scenic tour of Zurich combined with a delicious fondue meal. Guests can sit back, relax, and enjoy the city's sights while savoring a pot of fondue with fresh bread and potatoes.
Cost: Tickets generally range from CHF 85-100 per person, which includes the fondue and the tram ride.

Chäsalp Restaurant:
Located on the outskirts of Zurich, Chäsalp is a cozy mountain hut-style restaurant that specializes in all things cheese. With several varieties of fondue and raclette, Chäsalp is an ideal spot for those looking to immerse themselves in Swiss culinary traditions.
Cost: Fondue prices start around CHF 30 per person.

Raclette Stube:
This quaint spot in Zurich's Old Town serves traditional raclette with all the classic accompaniments, including potatoes, pickles, and onions. The rustic, alpine-inspired ambiance adds to the authentic Swiss dining experience.
Cost: Raclette is typically priced between CHF 25-35.

New Year's Eve Celebrations and Fireworks

Zurich's New Year's Eve celebrations are known for their vibrant energy and stunning fireworks display over Lake Zurich, organized by the Zurich Hoteliers' Association. The event draws large crowds to the lakefront, where people gather to welcome the new year with music, food stalls, and a grand midnight fireworks show.

Event Highlights:
The celebration begins with live music performances and DJ sets at various venues along the lake. Food and drink stalls offer hot mulled wine, Swiss sausages, and other festive treats. At midnight, fireworks light up the sky over Lake Zurich, creating a beautiful spectacle that reflects off the water. The best spots to view the fireworks are along the lake promenade, especially near Bürkliplatz and Bellevue.

Tips for Attending:

- Arrive early to secure a good viewing spot, as it gets crowded closer to midnight.

- Dress warmly, as temperatures can drop significantly in the winter.

- Public transport runs extended hours on New Year's Eve, making it easy to return to your accommodation after the festivities.

Zurich's winter attractions offer a blend of charm, culture, and seasonal delights, making the city an enchanting place to visit during the colder months. Whether wandering through festive markets, savoring traditional Swiss dishes, or taking in breathtaking winter landscapes, there's no shortage of things to do and see. For visitors, Zurich in winter promises an unforgettable experience filled with warmth, tradition, and joy.

Zurich's Unique Local Traditions

Zurich, with its rich history and vibrant cultural life, is home to several traditions that give visitors a deeper insight into the city's character. From unique festivals to local customs, Zurich's traditions reflect its Swiss heritage while offering a distinct local flavor. Experiencing these customs, especially around specific times of the year, can reveal Zurich's cultural soul and make a visit all the more memorable.

Sechseläuten: Welcoming Spring with a Fiery Celebration

Sechseläuten is one of Zurich's most cherished traditions, dating back to the 16th century. Celebrated on the third Monday of April, this festival marks the symbolic end of winter and the arrival of spring. Zurich's guilds, historical associations representing different trades, play a central role in the festivities, with each guild participating in a colorful procession through the city.

The Böögg Burning:
The highlight of Sechseläuten is the burning of the Böögg, an effigy of a snowman symbolizing winter, which is filled with explosives. The Böögg is placed atop a large bonfire on Sechseläutenplatz, and as the fire climbs, anticipation builds. The quicker the Böögg's head explodes, the warmer and sunnier the upcoming summer is predicted to be. Thousands of locals and tourists gather to witness this unique spectacle, which blends tradition with an element of suspense. The event captures Zurich's sense of community, with people celebrating in local squares, parks, and along the banks of Lake Zurich.

Guild Parades
Zurich's historic guilds, each represented by costumed members, march through the streets in a lively procession. Wearing traditional attire and carrying banners, they honor Zurich's medieval past. Some guild members ride horses or carriages, while marching bands add to the vibrant atmosphere. The guilds often represent trades that were historically significant, such as bakers, butchers, and blacksmiths, connecting modern Zurich to its industrial roots.

Knabenschiessen: Youth Target Shooting Festival

Dating back to the 17th century, Knabenschiessen is another unique Zurich tradition. Held each September, it is a target shooting competition specifically for Zurich's youth, especially teenagers. Originally open only to boys (hence the name, meaning "boys shooting"), the event has been inclusive of both boys and girls since 1991.

Shooting Competition:
The main event is a target shooting contest using small-caliber rifles, where Zurich's youth showcase their marksmanship skills. The tradition highlights Switzerland's historic emphasis on shooting sports and national defense. Competitors receive prizes for accuracy, and the best shooters can gain recognition within the community. The event takes place at the Albisgütli shooting range, which transforms into a festival grounds during Knabenschiessen.

Family-Friendly Festivities:
Knabenschiessen isn't just about shooting; it's a city-wide festival with carnival rides, games, food stalls, and entertainment for all ages. From classic Swiss treats like

bratwurst and raclette to fairground attractions, the event has something for everyone. The festival atmosphere makes it a family-friendly occasion and offers visitors an opportunity to immerse themselves in a lesser-known Zurich tradition that emphasizes local community bonds.

Fasnacht: Zurich's Vibrant Carnival

Although Basel and Lucerne are better known for their Fasnacht (carnival) celebrations, Zurich has its own version of this vibrant festival, typically taking place in late February or early March. Fasnacht is a pre-Lenten celebration that allows Zurich residents to dress up, let loose, and enjoy street parades, music, and parties.

Costumes and Masks:
During Fasnacht, people dress in elaborate costumes and masks that can range from funny to frightening, giving Zurich's streets a surreal and colorful look. Traditional Swiss masks, often crafted by hand, are worn by participants who parade through the streets, playing musical instruments or performing skits. The use of costumes and masks symbolizes a temporary escape from social norms, with people often using the opportunity to playfully mock authority or social conventions.

Guggenmusik (Brass Bands):
A defining feature of Fasnacht is the Guggenmusik bands, where musicians play lively and sometimes intentionally out-of-tune brass music. These bands perform traditional songs as well as contemporary pop hits, infusing the festival with an atmosphere of joyful chaos. The parades led by Guggenmusik bands march through Zurich's main squares, including

Münsterhof and Bellevue, creating an infectious party-like atmosphere.

Fasnacht gives visitors a chance to see a wilder side of Zurich, with people of all ages joining the festivities, dancing in the streets, and enjoying traditional Swiss treats from vendors along the parade routes.

Räbeliechtli: The Lantern Parade for Children

Räbeliechtli, or the Turnip Lantern Festival, is a charming tradition that takes place in November, when the days are getting shorter. Celebrated primarily by young children, Räbeliechtli involves carving turnips (Swiss chard) into lanterns and parading through the city in the evening, singing traditional songs and illuminating the streets with soft, warm lights.

Turnip Carving and Lantern Making:
Schools, families, and communities across Zurich spend the weeks leading up to Räbeliechtli carving turnips into intricate lanterns. Similar to pumpkins at Halloween, the carved designs on the turnips allow candlelight to shine through, creating a beautiful, glowing effect. Children carry their handmade lanterns and sing songs that celebrate nature and the harvest season, fostering a sense of tradition and community. This practice reflects Zurich's connection to Swiss agricultural roots and the importance of seasonal change.

Neighborhood Parades:
Neighborhoods throughout Zurich organize small parades where children walk with their lanterns, often accompanied by parents and teachers. The sight of glowing turnip lanterns lining Zurich's streets creates a warm, festive atmosphere,

even on chilly autumn evenings. The festival usually concludes with warm drinks and treats like hot chocolate or gingerbread cookies, making it a cherished family tradition.

Räbeliechtli is particularly heartwarming for visitors, who can witness Zurich's focus on tradition, family, and community in this uniquely Swiss celebration.

Samichlaus Day: The Swiss Saint Nicholas Tradition

Samichlaus Day, celebrated on December 6, is the Swiss version of Saint Nicholas Day, a holiday marking the start of the Christmas season. In Zurich, children eagerly await Samichlaus (the Swiss Santa Claus), who visits homes, schools, and town squares to bring gifts and sweets to well-behaved children. Samichlaus is usually accompanied by Schmutzli, his helper dressed in dark clothing.

Traditional Gifts and Sweets:
Instead of bringing gifts on Christmas Day, Swiss families observe Samichlaus Day, when children receive small treats like tangerines, nuts, and gingerbread cookies from Samichlaus. He often recites rhyming verses about good behavior, encouraging children to be kind and helpful. Families prepare traditional Swiss treats, including Grittibänz (a bread figure shaped like a little man), which are enjoyed by children during the celebrations.

Visits to the Forest:
In Zurich, Samichlaus is often found in the local forest, where families can hike to meet him. Samichlaus sits in a designated area with Schmutzli, and families take turns sharing snacks, songs, and stories with him. This outdoor setting reflects

Swiss appreciation for nature and family-oriented holiday traditions.

Samichlaus Day provides an early taste of Zurich's festive season and offers visitors insight into Swiss customs surrounding family, discipline, and joy.

Zurich's unique traditions not only highlight its Swiss identity but also create memorable experiences that bring visitors closer to local culture. These celebrations, often involving families and entire neighborhoods, showcase Zurich's dedication to community, heritage, and seasonal change, inviting all who visit to join in the festivities and take part in Swiss customs that have been cherished for generations.

11

Where To Stay: Hotels, Hostels, And Apartments

Zurich offers a variety of accommodations, from luxury hotels to budget-friendly hostels and short-term apartment rentals. Selecting the right type of lodging depends on factors like budget, preferred amenities, and proximity to key attractions. Here's an extensive guide on where to stay in Zurich, covering various types of accommodations and some popular options within each category.

Luxury Hotels: Comfort, Elegance, and Prime Locations

Zurich has a selection of high-end hotels that provide top-notch amenities and are typically located near major attractions like Bahnhofstrasse, the Old Town, and Lake Zurich. Luxury hotels in Zurich are known for their exceptional service, elegant decor, and added touches, such as spas, gourmet dining options, and personalized concierge services.

Baur au Lac:
Location: Near Bahnhofstrasse, overlooking Lake Zurich.

This five-star hotel has been a staple in Zurich since 1844 and offers luxurious rooms and suites with stunning views of the lake and the Alps. Amenities include a gourmet restaurant, Pavillon, a Michelin-starred venue with a focus on seasonal ingredients.

Price Range: From around CHF 900 per night, though rates vary depending on the season and room type.

The Dolder Grand:
Location: On a hillside overlooking Zurich, offering panoramic views.

Known for its unique blend of classic and modern architecture, The Dolder Grand is a destination in itself. With world-class art collections, an award-winning spa, and a two-Michelin-starred restaurant, this hotel attracts travelers seeking an opulent stay.

Price Range: Starts from approximately CHF 700 per night.

Hotel Schweizerhof Zürich:
Location: Directly across from Zurich's main train station, Zürich Hauptbahnhof.

This luxury hotel combines historic charm with modern comforts, offering spacious rooms and suites and fine dining options. It's ideal for those who want to stay close to transport links while enjoying luxury amenities.

Price Range: Around CHF 500 per night and up.

Mid-Range Hotels: Comfort and Value

For travelers who want comfortable accommodations without the expense of five-star amenities, Zurich has several mid-range hotels that offer good value for money. These options are generally well-located, offering easy access to public transportation and popular attractions.

Hotel City Zürich:
Location: Near Bahnhofstrasse, close to the Old Town.
This three-star hotel offers modern and well-equipped rooms, making it a great choice for travelers looking for comfort and convenience. Guests appreciate the hotel's stylish decor and friendly service.
Price Range: Rates start around CHF 200 per night.

Sorell Hotel Zürichberg:
Location: A hillside location offering views of Zurich and Lake Zurich.
Part of the Sorell hotel group, this boutique hotel provides a peaceful setting surrounded by greenery. It features contemporary design, comfortable rooms, and a restaurant with Swiss and international cuisine.
Price Range: From CHF 180 per night.

Boutique Hotel NI-MO:
Location: In Zurich's Seefeld district, close to Lake Zurich.
A small and charming hotel with an emphasis on personal service, NI-MO offers cozy rooms and a daily breakfast buffet. The hotel's location near the lake and opera house makes it a convenient option for sightseeing.
Price Range: Typically around CHF 150–200 per night.

Budget Hotels and Hostels: Affordable Options for Budget Travelers

While Zurich is known for its high cost of living, budget-conscious travelers can find affordable accommodations, especially in hostels and select budget hotels. These options offer the essentials—clean rooms, helpful amenities, and access to shared spaces—at a more reasonable price.
Zurich Youth Hostel:

Location: About 10 minutes from Zurich's main train station by tram.

This is one of Zurich's most popular hostels, offering shared and private rooms with basic facilities. It has a communal kitchen, lounge areas, and outdoor seating, making it easy to socialize with other travelers.

Price Range: Dorm beds start around CHF 40, while private rooms are available from CHF 90.

Oldtown Hostel Otter:

Location: Situated in Zurich's Old Town, close to the lake and main attractions.

A comfortable and friendly hostel with dormitories and a few private rooms. The hostel has a lively atmosphere, a bar, and an outdoor terrace.

Price Range: Dorm beds from CHF 50; private rooms start around CHF 100.

Hotel St. Georges:

Location: In the lively Wiedikon neighborhood, just a short tram ride from the city center.

This two-star hotel offers affordable, cozy rooms and friendly service. It's ideal for budget travelers who prefer the privacy of a hotel room over a hostel.

Price Range: Prices range from CHF 100 to CHF 130 per night.

Apartment Rentals: Flexibility and a Home-Like Stay

Renting an apartment can be a cost-effective and comfortable option for travelers, particularly those planning a longer stay. Apartments offer additional space, kitchen facilities, and the convenience of living like a local. Short-term apartment rentals are available through platforms like Airbnb and Vrbo, as well as local agencies.

Family and Group Stays:
Zurich's apartments can range from small studios to multi-room spaces, accommodating families and groups. Look for apartments in neighborhoods like Seefeld, Enge, and Wipkingen for easy access to public transport and a quieter atmosphere.
Price Range: Studio apartments typically start around CHF 120 per night, while larger apartments for families or groups can range from CHF 200 to CHF 400 per night.

Business Apartments:
Zurich also has a range of business apartments that cater to corporate travelers. These apartments are often in the city center and come fully equipped with high-speed internet, workspaces, and laundry facilities.
Price Range: From CHF 150 to CHF 300 per night, depending on size and location.

Tips for Choosing Accommodation in Zurich

Consider Proximity to Public Transport:
Zurich's neighborhoods are well-connected by trams, buses, and trains. If you're staying a bit outside the city center, being close to a tram stop or train station will make it easy to get around.

Book Early for Peak Seasons:
Zurich's high season runs from June to August, and prices can rise significantly. The Christmas season, with its holiday markets and events, is also busy. Booking early can help secure better rates.

Neighborhoods to Consider:

- Altstadt (Old Town): Ideal for those who want to be close to Zurich's historic sites, restaurants, and nightlife.

- Zurich West: Known for its trendy atmosphere, Zurich West is filled with art galleries, music venues, and unique dining options.

- Seefeld: A quieter, residential area close to the lake, Seefeld is great for families and travelers seeking a scenic environment.

Whether travelers are drawn to the comforts of a luxury hotel, the affordability of a hostel, or the independence of an apartment rental, Zurich's diverse accommodation options cater to a range of preferences.

Money Matters: Currency, Tipping, And Budget Tips

Traveling to Zurich means navigating a high-cost city, but understanding local customs around currency, tipping, and budgeting can help visitors manage their expenses. Here's an overview to help you make the most of your money during your trip.

Currency in Zurich

Switzerland uses the Swiss Franc (CHF), symbolized as "CHF" or sometimes "Fr." This currency is accepted throughout Zurich, and it's worth noting that while some places near the border may accept Euros, they'll often do so at a less favorable exchange rate. Credit and debit cards are widely accepted in Zurich, especially in hotels, restaurants, and major retail stores, but it's always a good idea to carry some cash for small purchases, especially at local markets or in smaller establishments.

Exchange Rates:
The Swiss Franc is generally stable but can fluctuate based on international markets. It's recommended to check exchange rates before your trip to better plan your budget.

Where to Exchange Currency:

- Banks: Zurich's banks offer currency exchange services, though they may charge a small fee.

- ATMs: ATMs are easy to find in Zurich, and many offer fair exchange rates for withdrawing local currency directly. However, check with your bank about foreign transaction fees.

- Currency Exchange Offices: You'll find these at the Zurich Airport and some tourist areas. Though convenient, they often come with higher fees.

Tipping Etiquette in Zurich

Tipping in Zurich is appreciated but not mandatory, as Swiss law requires that service charges be included in prices at restaurants, hotels, and taxis. However, leaving a small tip is common and viewed as a friendly gesture.

Restaurants:
It's typical to round up the bill or add 5–10% as a gratuity for good service. For example, if your meal costs CHF 47, you could leave CHF 50. High-end restaurants may warrant a slightly larger tip, but it's not expected.

Bars:
Tipping at bars follows similar rules. Rounding up is common, though some locals simply say "keep the change" on smaller purchases.

Hotels:
A small tip is appreciated for excellent service. Porters may be tipped CHF 1–2 per bag, while housekeeping staff can be given CHF 2–5 per day if they've provided exceptional service.

Taxis:

In Zurich, taxi drivers do not expect a tip, but rounding up to the next franc or adding a small amount (5–10%) is a courteous gesture.

Budget Tips for Zurich

Zurich is an expensive city, but with a few strategies, travelers can enjoy the city's offerings without breaking the bank. Here are some tips to help manage costs:

Zurich Card:
Purchasing a Zurich Card can be a great way to save on transportation and sightseeing. The card provides unlimited travel on public transport within Zurich, discounts at select museums, and special offers on tours and activities.
Cost: CHF 27 for 24 hours or CHF 53 for 72 hours.
Benefits: Besides transportation savings, the card offers free or discounted admission to popular attractions, making it ideal for visitors planning to explore museums and other sites.

Eating Smart:

- Supermarkets and Food Courts: Switzerland's grocery stores, such as Coop and Migros, offer fresh food options at lower prices than restaurants. Some Coop City locations have food courts with affordable meals, and takeaway sandwiches or salads can save on dining costs.

- Ethnic Restaurants: Zurich has a range of international cuisine that's often more budget-friendly than traditional Swiss dining. Asian, Middle Eastern, and Italian eateries tend to offer reasonable prices.

- Lunch Specials: Many restaurants offer set lunch menus, providing quality meals at lower prices than dinner. Look out for "Mittagsmenu" (lunch menu) deals at cafes and bistros around town.

Free or Affordable Activities:

- Walking Tours: Zurich's Old Town, riverbanks, and parks are ideal for self-guided walking tours. Sites like the Lindenhof Hill and Lake Zurich Promenade are free to visit and showcase the city's beauty.

- Museum Free Days: Some museums offer free admission on certain days or times. For example, Kunsthaus Zürich is free on Wednesdays, and the Swiss National Museum has reduced rates for students and seniors.

- Explore Nature: Natural attractions like Uetliberg Mountain and Lake Zurich are free to access and offer breathtaking views and hiking trails.

Public Transportation:
Zurich's public transport system is efficient and budget-friendly, especially with a day pass or the Zurich Card. Avoid taxis, which are significantly more expensive, and opt for trams, buses, or trains.

By planning ahead, taking advantage of local deals, and understanding Zurich's tipping culture, travelers can enjoy a rewarding experience in Zurich without overspending. Balancing a few budget strategies with occasional splurges allows visitors to enjoy Zurich's rich offerings comfortably.

Language, Etiquette, And Local Customs

To fully appreciate Zurich's charm, it helps to understand a bit about the local language, etiquette, and customs. A few key insights can go a long way in making your interactions smoother and your visit more immersive.

Language in Zurich

Zurich is primarily a German-speaking city, and Swiss German, or "Schwiizerdütsch," is the local dialect. While the dialect can sound quite different from standard German, most residents also understand and speak High German (Hochdeutsch), making it easier for German speakers to communicate. English is widely spoken, especially in tourist areas, shops, and restaurants, so visitors will find it relatively easy to navigate Zurich without knowing German. However, locals appreciate even small efforts to speak German, and learning a few simple phrases can help make a positive impression:

- Hello: Hallo
- Thank you: Danke
- Please: Bitte
- Excuse me: Entschuldigung
- Goodbye: Auf Wiedersehen (formal), Tschüss (informal)

Etiquette and Manners

Swiss culture values punctuality, politeness, and respect for privacy, so observing these standards in Zurich will help you feel at ease. Here are some key points:

Greetings:
Handshakes are a standard way to greet people, especially in formal situations. If you're introduced to someone new, a friendly handshake and eye contact show respect. Among close friends or family, a kiss on the cheek—often done three times—is customary.

Punctuality:
Punctuality is highly valued in Switzerland, whether for social gatherings, appointments, or tours. Arriving late, even by a few minutes, may be seen as disrespectful, so aim to be on time or even a few minutes early.

Quietness:
Swiss people appreciate a quiet atmosphere, especially in public spaces like trams, buses, and trains. Speaking in a low tone in public and avoiding loud behavior will be appreciated by locals. This respect for quiet extends to hotels and residential areas, where noise ordinances are strictly observed, especially in the evenings.

Public Transportation Etiquette:
When boarding Zurich's trams, buses, or trains, it's polite to let passengers exit before entering. If the vehicle is crowded, be considerate of others by keeping personal belongings close to you and offering your seat to elderly or disabled individuals.

Dining Customs:

When dining out, it's courteous to greet your server with a polite "Guten Tag" (Good day) or "Grüezi" (Hello). If dining in a group, waiting for everyone to receive their food before beginning to eat is customary. It's also common to say "En Guete" (enjoy your meal) to your dining companions before starting.

Local Customs and Traditions

Zurich holds a deep appreciation for its history and traditions, many of which are unique to Switzerland:

Sunday Rest:
Sundays in Zurich are reserved for rest and relaxation. Most shops and businesses are closed, allowing residents to spend time with family, take leisurely walks, or enjoy outdoor activities. You'll find Zurich a bit quieter on Sundays, and visitors often use this day to enjoy parks, museums, and cafes, which remain open.

Recycling and Cleanliness:
Zurich is known for its cleanliness, and this is partly due to the city's strict recycling policies and pride in public spaces. Recycling bins are widely available, and residents are encouraged to separate waste carefully. Following these practices shows respect for the city and its residents.

Cultural Celebrations:
Zurich has many traditional festivals and events that offer insight into Swiss culture. One of the unique customs is Sechseläuten, a spring festival celebrated with the burning of the Böögg, a snowman effigy, to symbolize the end of winter. If visiting during such events, feel free to join in, as locals are usually welcoming and happy to share their traditions.

As your journey through Zurich concludes, remember that the city's essence lies in its blend of tradition and innovation. From the rich architecture of the Old Town to the quiet shores of Lake Zurich, this city is a mosaic of experiences shaped by history, respect, and a sense of community. By observing local customs, you become part of Zurich's fabric, discovering not just a destination but a place that feels like a second home.

May Zurich leave you inspired, enriched, and eager to return. Safe travels, and may the memories you make here be as vibrant as the city itself.

Made in the USA
Las Vegas, NV
15 December 2024

14314208R00105